making
disciples

# one

# conversation

# at a

# time

d. michael henderson

BEACON HILL PRESS
OF KANSAS CITY

Copyright 2007
By D. Michael Henderson and Beacon Hill Press of Kansas City

ISBN-13: 978-0-8341-2300-7
ISBN-10: 0-8341-2300-2

Cover Design: Chad A Cherry
Interior Design: Sharon Page

**Library of Congress Cataloging-in-Publication Data**

Henderson, D. Michael.
   Making disciples— one conversation at a time / D. Michael Henderson.
      p. cm.
   ISBN-13: 978-0-8341-2300-7 (pbk.)
   ISBN-10: 0-8341-2300-2 (pbk.)
   1. Discipling (Christianity) 2. Conversation—Religious aspects—Christianity. I. Title.

   BV4520.H455 2007
   253'.7—dc22

                                                                                 2006103317

10 9 8 7 6 5 4 3 2 1

# Contents

118448

My life has
been shaped
by conversations
with my friends,
to whom I dedicate
this book.

Among them are
Van Graham
Terry Schaberg
Rolf Garborg
Mark Royster

I would
(and do)
travel halfway
across the country
for a chat with
any one of them.

# introduction

The kingdom of God spreads throughout the world one conversation at a time. The art of making disciples is the art of redemptive discussion. You make disciples one conversation at a time. Just as you began following Jesus at some point in your life, you make disciples by helping your friends do the same. Conversation by conversation you help your friend take the next step, then the next, then the next, until he or she not only reflects the character of Jesus inwardly but also takes the initiative to help someone else follow.

Jesus announced the coming of the kingdom of God to large masses of people. Many were intrigued by His teachings and stories. But most of those people did not become His disciples. Only a faithful few became genuine followers of the Master. He spent the majority of His time talking with those few, His disciples, and He entrusted the ongoing establishment of His kingdom, the Church, to them. He gave them His *great commission,* which was to go into all the world and make disciples; apparently they did, because the Kingdom has now spread to every part of the globe.

We, too, are entrusted with that same commission: to make disciples. How will we accomplish that assignment? By mass meetings, publicity campaigns, television campaigns, and catchy slogans? Not if we follow His example.

We have to learn to make disciples one discussion, one conversation, one heart-to-heart discussion at a time.

Barnabas was one of the great disciple-makers of the Early Church. He specialized in those hard cases that nobody else would touch, like Saul, who had been a notorious persecutor of Christians, and John Mark, who was a quitter. He patiently encouraged them in their walk with Christ so that both of them became outstanding Christian leaders. You can do the same with those hard cases among your circle of friends.

We are tempted (and encouraged) to believe that the kingdom of God spreads throughout the earth by presenting the gospel, through some pat formula, to total strangers. That doesn't happen very often. The gospel spread throughout the world of the first centuries by conversations between close friends and relatives, business associates and neighbors—people with whom the passionate Christians already had personal contact. So today the Church grows and expands, and people come to maturity in Christ nearly always through the influence of people they already know and trust, like you.

Even the most shy person among us talks to people every day. Most of that talk is idle chatter, not very useful for the advancement of God's kingdom. Every one of those less-than-redemptive conversations is a lost opportunity for extending the Lordship of Jesus. However, if we could learn to enhance the quality of our conversations, we could improve our ability to do what Jesus commanded—make disciples. We could turn that meaningless chatter into a means of God's grace, helping our friends become all God intends for them and enriching their lives (and our own) in the process.

The purpose of this book is to help all of us do better in assisting our friends to follow Jesus. We can come to the place where we can say with Paul, the great apostle, "Follow my example, as I follow the example of Christ" (1 Cor. 11:1). I want to present simple steps any Christian can follow to turn everyday talk into spiritual growth. It's all built around our most precious human commodity: friendships. Making a disciple is nothing more than helping our friends follow Jesus, and we do that by sanctifying our words so they do some good.

# what is

# Jesus

## doing right

# now?

You know what Jesus did 2,000 years ago, and you believe strongly enough in what He did to commit yourself to following Him. But an even more important thought for you today is this: What is Jesus doing right now, this very moment, and what should I be doing today to help Him?

One thing He is doing right now is interceding for us. He is seated at the right hand of God, receiving our worship and making our needs known to the Father—and only He can do that; we can't help. He is also preparing a place for us—and we can't help with that, either. He isn't taking requests concerning our eternal accommodations. However, we can and should have an active role in His current work of establishing His kingdom on earth, which is the same as building His Church.

Many Christians live their lives as though Jesus finished His work in the first century. They seem to think that being a Christian is simply accepting the finished work of Christ, going to church every Sunday to express their worship, and waiting for His second coming. No, no, no. Jesus is working today, just as He did 2,000 years ago, to accomplish His cosmic mission. Long before the first humans made their appearance, He was busy creating the universe. Perhaps He still is. At a certain time in history God poured His energy into the earthly ministry of Jesus. And since then He has been actively working in the affairs of people to bring humanity under the Lordship of His kingdom.

Somehow people can't grasp the idea that Jesus goes to work every day, just like we do. Or conversely, and more correctly, we go to work every day, just like Jesus does. He told His disciples, "My father is always at his work to this very day, and I, too, am working" (John 5:17). He still is.

The central task of the universe today is extending the kingdom of God into every corner of human life, one follower at a time, one conversation at a time. That's what Jesus is concentrating on, and that's what we should be spending the best part of our time and energy doing. You may have assumed that the most important thing you could be doing with your life is selling carpet in Centerville, raising kids in Indiana, governing the state of Louisiana, discovering a cure for cancer, or pastoring the second-largest church in a small town. Those are all worthwhile endeavors, but each one of those tasks is only significant when it is a subtask of the grand objective: building the kingdom of God.

After Jesus completed the earthly segment of establishing His kingdom, He gathered His friends around Him and laid out the strategy for the next phase. His friends weren't very mature, spiritually, at the time of this meeting; in fact some of them still doubted. However, in spite of their immaturity Jesus delegated the next phase of the expansion of the Kingdom to them. It was to be a joint venture; in partnership with Jesus' own Spirit, they were assigned to make disciples of the whole world, following the plan of Kingdom growth Jesus had modeled for them— one disciple at a time, one step at a time. And He gave them a blank check—drawn on all the resources of heaven—to accomplish this next step in the Kingdom's establishment. There was only one limitation: these resources were for making disciples only.

Just as the task of recording the revelation of God through the centuries had been delegated to individual people with the assistance of the Holy Spirit, even so Jesus delegated the spread of the gospel to His friends. Since we are His friends, we have that same assignment. And we also have the same promise: that He will be with us in every step of that enterprise.

So if we are sent by Jesus Christ to make disciples in our world, we'd better know for sure what a disciple is. And once we know that, we need to figure out how to make more of them.

Disciples are simply people who follow Jesus. At some point in their lives they have accepted His claim to be the Son of God, the one person in the universe worthy of following. In most cases disciples have had to turn away from less worthy pursuits and go a different direction. For some people, following Jesus is something they have done for as long as they can remember. For others it is a radically new idea. The important issue is not how a person got started on this pilgrimage but whether he or she is currently following Jesus. "Following Jesus" today simply means taking the same steps Jesus instructed His first-century friends to take, the steps so clearly recorded in the New Testament.

Those first-century disciples enjoyed their friendship

with Jesus. They walked along with Him, talking about things they saw on the way. He taught them practical lessons about God's kingdom, using life experiences as illustrations. That's what being a disciple means today: enjoying companionship with Jesus, learning from Him about the Kingdom, and taking whatever step we see Him taking ahead of us. It doesn't matter where we joined the journey, just that we are following.

In the process of following Jesus, an amazing transformation takes place: the follower becomes more and more like the leader. The Holy Spirit shapes and bends the character of His followers until they, too, have the mind of Christ and do the kinds of good things that their leader did. These steps are not the ultimate objective; the goal is to become like Christ.

A kingdom is the territory under the control of a king. Earthly kings mark out that territory in geographic terms: from the river on that side to the mountains on this side. But the territory God seeks to control is human hearts. His kingdom is all those hearts loyal to King Jesus. That Kingdom is penetrating more and more of our world as people surrender to His Kingship and place more and more of their lives under His authority. It is spreading throughout the world in an inevitable and unstoppable tide that cannot be suppressed and will not be thwarted. The only question for us and our friends is, "Will we ride the wave or be swept under by it?"

Jesus did not come to sell memberships in the King-

dom. Only religious hucksters do that. He merely announced that with His arrival God's kingdom had come.
Those who follow Him will enjoy it and its privileges.
Those who don't are going the wrong way. "Repent!" He
said. "Turn around! You're going the wrong direction. I'm
the truth, the way, the life. Follow Me. There's no future
the other way." Jesus didn't make any effort to coerce or
cajole people into the Kingdom. In fact He raised the bar
high enough that only those who really are serious about
following Him will find that Kingdom.

If a disciple is simply a follower of Jesus, how complicated can making disciples be? To make a disciple is
simply to help our friends follow Jesus, one intimate discussion at a time. Making disciples is having helpful conversations with our friends, helping them take the next
step in following Jesus.

Sometimes it is our privilege to help one of our
friends take the first step in the journey with Christ: the
step of initial faith. This can be a moment of high drama
or a long process of growing acceptance of Jesus as King
of Eternity. The logistics of this step are not as important
as the fact of it. Just because you came to faith in Christ in
a certain manner doesn't mean that all your friends will
have the same experience, or that any of them will.

Martha and I were sitting in church recently, getting
ready to receive the elements of Communion, the Lord's
Supper. Our worship leader said, "This is a family meal.
It's only for family members. If you haven't joined God's

family, you shouldn't participate. However, if you are on the outside looking in and want to be included in God's family, there are people at the back of the room who will help you take the next step. Then you can join us in the family celebration."

A young couple in the row ahead of us were having a serious whisper about something, and I sensed that the husband was ready to take his first step of faith. Sure enough, he got up from his seat and made his way to the back. As he passed the sound booth, one of our tech guys asked him, "What do you need?" Scott, the young husband, said, "Jesus." The technician pointed him to Ralph, one of the mature Christians waiting in the back, who helped him take the first steps in a life of walking with Jesus. Scott's wife had also come to join him, as I had, and we gathered around him as he prayed. Now Scott and Ralph get together on a fairly regular basis, and Scott is making great progress as a follower of Jesus.

Sometimes we help our friends take the last step. My Aunt, Peg Henderson, was one of Jesus' sweetest followers. Her whole life was spent in gracious service to her family, friends, church, neighbors, and colleagues at work. Last year we moved to Florida, just a few miles from Aunt Peg and nearer than any of her own kids or grandkids. So we had lots of enjoyable visits with her, although some of them involved trips to the hospital for her deteriorating health. In May she went into the hospital for the last time.

It was clear to us and to her that she was taking her last step with Jesus in this life.

Martha and I had the bittersweet joy of helping Aunt Peg take her last step. All her kids and grandkids gathered around her bedside for several days, and finally it was time for her to tell them all good-bye. She gave each one a blessing, and when she got too tired to stay awake she said, "I'm going to sleep, and when I wake up I'll be in heaven." And so she did, and we were gratified that we had helped a grand Christian lady take her last step and take it well.

Making a disciple is teaching your friend to learn from the Holy Spirit. You're not the teacher; you're just a friend. Jesus promised that when He was no longer physically present with His disciples He would send the Holy Spirit to teach, guide, comfort, and correct them and help them stay on track. Our role in that process is to help our friends stay tuned in to the Spirit and to walk, step by step, in a divinely led pilgrimage. We do that by talking: discussing, holding accountable, sometimes confronting, encouraging, asking good questions, and so on. Human interaction is how the kingdom of God spreads. Friends talk to friends, steps are taken in following Jesus, and His Kingship oozes into more and more of human life. The Holy Spirit, through human agents, is conquering new territory all the time, building allegiance and loyalty to Jesus in the hearts of His people and helping them do things His way.

Together, friends do God's work in the world. When

Jesus said, "Go into all the world and make disciples" (see Matt. 28:19; Mark 16:15), He meant the corner of the world you live in. Establish God's kingdom right there. You and your friends are colleagues in a conspiracy of kindness to do good things in Jesus' name. In your circle of influence you are channels of God's grace and power to bring truth and justice, love and compassion, peace and harmony, one conversation at a time. As the old poem goes, "Little drops of water, / Little grains of sand, / Make the mighty ocean and the beauteous land. / Little deeds of kindness, / Little words of love, / Make our earth an Eden / Like the heaven above" (Mrs. J. A. Carney).

Obviously, we can't extend the kingdom of God in our own strength. It would be the height of arrogance to even think we could. But in partnership with God's Spirit, all He asked us to do is entirely possible. I know there are people who try to do good on their own, in their own strength, but it's a futile effort.

One of my favorite stories is about a vacuum cleaner salesman making calls in the mountains of eastern Kentucky. He drove up into the head of a hollow and knocked on the door of a mountain cabin. When the lady of the house answered the door, he pushed his way inside without even giving her a chance to say "howdy" and dumped a large bag of dirt on her linoleum floor. "Madam," he announced, "if my Ace Vacuum Cleaner can't suck all this dirt up in one minute, I'll give you $20.00!" To this the woman replied, "Good luck, Sonny. We ain't got no 'lectric!"

That's what we say to those noble do-gooders who are trying to save the world in their own strength: "Good luck, Sonny! You've got the right idea but no power." Those of us who are following Jesus are on a mission to make our world a better place by making disciples and doing God's work, and He has given us the authority and resources to transform our own little corner of the world.

As the writer of the Book of Hebrews reminded us, "Therefore, since we are receiving a kingdom which cannot be shaken, let us have grace, by which we may serve God acceptably with reverence and godly fear. For our God is a consuming fire" (12:28-29, NKJV).

## For Reflection and Discussion

1. What is Jesus doing right now?

2. How is His kingdom spreading throughout the world?

3. What is a disciple? And what does it mean to "make disciples"?

4. In the process of making disciples, who is supposed to be the teacher?

# laying

# down

## your life

# for your

# Friends

Jesus showed us how to make disciples. He not only taught us the content of His instruction but gave us the method as well. As we will examine in fuller detail in a later chapter, the Bible is not only our message book but also our *method* book. Many churches claim to be Bible-believing, but their orthodoxy extends only to the content of their belief system, not their methodology. In that sense, they are only half-biblical. Consequently, they are seldom successful in making genuine disciples.

The method Jesus taught us is simple: help our friends follow Him. Encourage them to put into practice all He taught us about the kingdom of God. Jesus built His instructional system on the basis of His own personal friendships. He chose men to be His followers who were not only His friends but also already friends, relatives, and neighbors of each other. They were bound together by ties of familiarity, blood relationships, and hearty companionship—and most of them worked together every day. Before they began learning the principles of God's kingdom there was already a strong foundation of loyalty, affection, and brotherly commitment among them.

Jesus chose James and John, the sons of Zebedee, who were brothers and fishermen on the Sea of Galilee. Simon, who later became known as Peter, was Andrew's brother, and they were fishermen on the same lake. Andrew and Philip were friends. The other apostle named James and Matthew the tax-collector were brothers. John the Baptist was Jesus' own cousin. Jesus established His

Church, the kingdom of God on earth, on the groundwork of the intimate relationships that already existed among His friends.

Now, you have chosen to follow Jesus, and you have some friends. Why not build on those relationships you already have to carry out the mission Jesus has given you? Why not help your friends take the next step in following Jesus? That would make you a disciple-maker, and you would be fulfilling His great commission.

Most of us will never have the privilege of laying down our physical lives for our friends. However, if we really love them, we will lay down the most precious commodities of our life for their spiritual welfare: our time, our resources, and our convenience. I know you wouldn't hesitate a second to help your friend if he or she were in danger or distress. You have probably already made great sacrifices to see that your family or neighbors get every advantage. Why is it different to help them attain the greatest blessing of all: spiritual maturity and effectiveness in service to others?

Jesus boldly affirmed His affection for His disciples by saying, "Greater love has no one than this, that he lay down his life for his friends" (John 15:13). Then He did it. He deliberately faced a cruel death on the Cross that they might receive all God had for them. Astonishing as this may seem to us, this pleased His Heavenly Father. Jesus said, "The reason my Father loves me is that I lay down my life" (10:17). God is pleased with us when we demonstrate our love for our friends in the same way.

I was proud of my kids when they learned to ride a bike, made good grades in school, and did well in sports. But my greatest joy has come as I have watched each of them, and their spouses, make great and painful sacrifices to help their friends follow Christ. Although I don't wish any pain to come to my children, I am pleased when they make great sacrifices on behalf of others, even if those efforts cost them personal loss, disappointment, and pain. I would grieve if they lost their lives in service to others, but I would also be the proudest father on earth.

Jesus is our ultimate model when it comes to investing our lives in our friends. However, there are other wonderful examples in Scripture of godly men and women helping their friends grow in their relationship to God. One striking example is Jonathan's mission to save the life of his friend David.

As recorded in 1 Sam. 23:15-18, David was running for his life from the armies of King Saul, Jonathan's father. At great risk to himself, Jonathan ventured into the Desert of Ziph to find David and warn him of Saul's plans. In that encounter, Jonathan did three things every man should learn to do for his friends: first, he encouraged David's heart in the Lord. David was convinced he was going to die, but Jonathan put his fears to rest. "'Don't be afraid,' he said. 'My father Saul will not lay a hand on you'" (v. 17). Jesus often had to say those very words to His disciples:

"Fear not!" Why? Because there were so many real dangers that provoked genuine fear, even in the hearts of those rugged outdoorsmen. Our friends are equally troubled by anxieties and distresses; we must learn how to come alongside them at fearful times and assure them that things are not as bad as they seem.

Second, Jonathan reminded David of God's promise: "You will be king over Israel" (v. 17). Again, that's what our friends need to hear—not that they will be kings but that God's promises to them will certainly come to pass. The more we know of God's promises, the more help we will be to them.

Third, Jonathan demonstrated his personal loyalty to David by "cutting a covenant" with him. If they followed standard Old Testament procedure, they cut their hands, mingled their blood, and swore their allegiance to each other. They may have drunk their commingled blood, as we do symbolically every time we "drink the covenant in his blood" (see 1 Cor. 11:25).

By doing these three things, Jonathan gave a gift of inestimable worth to his friend: the ability to encourage his heart in the Lord. Later, when David faced humiliating defeat and immobilizing fear, he was able to encourage his heart in the Lord (1 Sam. 30:3-9) because his friend Jonathan had shown him how. Think what strength would characterize Christians today if we knew how to practice that level of sacrificial, redemptive friendship!

Pastors often complain to me, "I can't get my congre-

disciples

are built

in the

Arena

of real

life.

gation to take discipleship classes." Of course you can't! Disciples are not made in either congregations or classes. I know. I've tried both. Those methods are not how Jesus showed us to make disciples. He didn't offer a course in the synagogue, take attendance, give lectures, and hand out reading assignments. He walked with His friends from place to place, using everyday experiences as the context for applying the principles of God's kingdom. He chose only 12 to be with Him, spent most of His time with 3 (Peter, James, and John), and explained many of the major truths of the Kingdom to just one disciple at a time. His classroom was life; His lessons were principles of the Kingdom they needed to know right then, right there.

Disciples grow in their walk with Christ in the context of personal friendship. If the friendship isn't there prior to the disciple-building process, then work on the friendship first. The relationship between friendship and discipleship is a two-edged sword: on the one hand, if you can't make friends, you certainly can't make disciples. On the other hand, if you are able to build friendships, you can easily learn to make disciples.

The setting is equally important. Disciples are built in the arena of real life. Christian character is molded in the experiences of everyday existence, situations at work, conflicts at home, opportunities in the neighborhood, and ministries in the local fellowship of believers. In 1977 I taught a college course on personal discipleship. I thought I was a genuine pioneer. Unfortunately I was just making the same mistake as many others who offer discipleship courses. The classroom is the wrong context because it is an artificial environment. And the relationship was wrong: I didn't have a prior friendship with those students, so I wasn't willing to lay down my life for them. They weren't my friends. They were my students. Their goal was knowledge (at best) and a good grade for the course.

If this is so, is there no place for formal instruction? Of course there is! The Kingdom advances on two wings: public teaching and private interaction. Jesus did both, and so should we. He taught the multitudes on the hillside, expounded the Scriptures in the synagogue, and announced the coming of the kingdom of heaven in all the towns and villages. But then He singled out those who proved themselves to be "doers of the word, and not hearers only" (James 1:22, NKJV), for personal mentoring. Today's Church has mastered the art of public proclamation in countless media: church services, radio and television, audiovisual techniques, courses, classes, and books. But the other wing of personal conversation has been neglected to the detriment of the central task of the Church: making disciples.

So, pastor, how do you introduce the mission of making disciples to your congregation? Here are some suggestions:

1.  Make disciples yourself. Don't encourage people to do what you're not doing. Here's an interesting observation: David, the giant killer, had at least four giant killers in his army (2 Sam. 21:18-22;

1 Chron. 20:4-8). Saul didn't have any giant killers in his army, because he had never killed a giant himself. You can't produce disciple-makers if you're not one yourself.

2. Make heroes of those people in your congregation who are helping their friends follow Jesus. If making disciples is the goal of your church, the congregation should hear stories every week of ordinary Christians who are out there on the front lines, helping their neighbors and relatives follow Jesus.

3. Encourage people to do the will of God. Strengthen their love for Christ. Challenge them to follow Jesus and obey Him. Then it won't be a huge step when they come to His command: "Make disciples . . . teaching them to obey everything I have commanded you" (Matt. 28:19-20).

4. Spend a lot of time training people to be good friends, good neighbors, and good family members. That's the foundation on which discipleship is built. Most churches don't produce very healthy disciples because they don't encourage healthy friendships.

5. Redefine what it means to be a Christian. Modern churches have accepted a watered-down caricature of Christianity that is designed to recruit members, not to train disciples. Jesus didn't say, "Raise your hand and you will be saved for eternity." He did

say, "Take up the cross, and follow Me" (Mark 10:21, NKJV). A Christian is one who is currently following Jesus and doing what He said to do.

In my own lifetime I have had a few great friends. I could count them on my hands. Those guys have stood by me through some very dark valleys. They didn't give up on me when I was convinced all hope was lost. There were times when they hurt me deeply by telling me the truth, and I love them for that. They laughed at my jokes and corrected my grammar. They prayed for my kids, and I prayed for theirs. We hunted together and went to ball games together, but we dug truth out of God's Word together too. They sent me tapes and books; I wrote them letters and clipped out helpful articles for them. We're pilgrims together, following Jesus and drawing other strugglers into our circle of friendship.

No, I'm not a self-made saint. I didn't pull myself up by my own bootstraps. I'm a disciple of Jesus by the grace of God and the loving investment of my friends. And I'm trying to do for others what my friends have done for me: help faithful people follow Jesus. That's what making disciples is all about.

## For Reflection and Discussion

1. What three things did Jonathan do for David that helped him deal with his problems?

2. What is the ultimate test of love?

3. Why is friendship the necessary relationship for genuine disciple-making to take place?

4. How does a pastor get started making disciples?

5. How did the first disciples know each other before they became followers of Jesus?

# keeping

# your eye

## on the

# goal:

# Christlikeness

Productive conversations have a clear objective. When you go to your doctor to discuss the results of your mammogram, you don't talk about the weather. You know why you're there, you ask pointed questions, and you get to the point. Why? Because it's your life you're discussing: whether you're going to be healthy and live or get sick and die.

Making disciples is serious business; it's a life-and-death issue. So when we talk to our friends about following Jesus we have to be clear about the goal. To keep myself on track I've chosen a goal statement from the apostle Paul as my standard for personal ministry. I've memorized Col. 1:28-29 in the paraphrase by J. B. Phillips that reads, "So, naturally, we proclaim Christ! We warn everyone we meet, and we teach everyone we can, all that we know about him, so that, if possible, we may bring every man up to his full maturity in Christ. This is what I am working at all the time, with all the strength God gives me."

What a powerful mission! To do all I can to help as many of my friends as possible attain full maturity in Christ. The goal is nothing less than Christlikeness—or, as Paul said to the Philippian Christians, having nothing less than the mind of Christ (see Phil. 2:1-11).

I'm sorry to say this goal is not universally shared among Christian leaders. Many seem to operate as though the goal is to get people saved, just to make sure they make it to heaven. That wasn't the goal Jesus set for us.

the

inward

objective

is Godly

character.

His desire is that His disciples follow Him, keep His commandments, and carry out the work of the Kingdom.

Most of us are familiar with Paul's wonderful statement about the authority of Scripture found in 2 Tim. 3:16. I learned it first in the King James Version: "All scripture is given by inspiration of God, and is profitable for doctrine, for reproof, for correction, for instruction in righteousness." That's a great statement of the trustworthiness and usefulness of the Bible. However, we often neglect the purpose for Scripture, the goal, which is located in the next verse: "That the man [or woman] of God may be perfect, throughly furnished unto all good works" (KJV).

The inward objective is godly character—nothing less than the thoughts, attitudes, and motivations of Jesus Christ himself. Yes, eternal life may begin in a moment, but the development of Christlike character is a lifetime pursuit. We can't be satisfied when our friends make professions of faith—that's just the beginning. The end toward which we must constantly push, both in ourselves and in the lives of our colleagues, is *full stature,* as Paul said in Eph. 4:13 (NRSV).

The external goal is equipping for service. Each of us must find our niche in the Body of Christ, then do those good works that God intends us to do. You may not be able to visualize your struggling new friend as a powerful worker in God's great harvest, but God does. You must develop the eyes of Jesus so you can perceive a great spiritual leader in a loud-mouthed, rash fisherman like Simon

Peter. You must be able to see a future bishop of Ephesus in a shy teenager like Timothy.

I got my best training listening to tapes. I used to check them out four at a time from Bible Believers' Cassettes in Springdale, Arkansas. I'd listen to them over and over, driving to school or work. I must have listened to Lorne Sanny's *Worth of the Individual* a hundred times, or Dawson Trotman's *Need of the Hour,* or Howard Hendricks' *Characteristics of a Leader.*

People sometimes ask me, "Where did you get your education?" I say, "On my way to Indiana University." I lived 75 miles from campus—just a long enough ride to listen to a good tape on the way to class and another one coming home. I'm sorry to say I didn't pick up much useful information at the university, but I learned a whole lot coming and going. One day I noticed the title of the tape, *Howard Hendricks' Personal Testimony.* Dr. Hendricks was one of my favorite speakers, although I only heard him on tape, and I assumed he must have just floated down from heaven as a fully developed seminary professor. I never would have guessed that he came from a troubled family and neighborhood.

I clicked the cassette into the tape player in my pickup and settled back for a pleasant presentation. I was so shocked by his testimony my eyes flooded with tears and I had to pull off the road to hear it all the way through. He came from a broken home in a slum in Philadelphia and started his story by saying, "Until I was 12 years old, nobody saw me as anything but a problem. But a Sunday School teacher named Walt loved 13 of us boys into the kingdom of God and built a foundation of godliness into our lives." For me, the most poignant statement he made was, "Walt saw us for what we could become, by God's grace."

That's the kind of vision an effective disciple-maker must have: the ability to see the finished product in the raw material. The ability to look at what everybody looks at and see what nobody sees. I thought about the people in my own church, some of whom lived up to young Howard Hendricks' standard: "nothing but a problem." I began praying that I would have the eyes of Jesus, to see in them the potential for both godly maturity and Christian leadership. It changed my whole perspective.

Some time later my senior pastor called me in. "I've got a problem," he said. "There's a guy in the class I'm trying to teach who constantly interrupts me. I told the class to raise their hands if they have a question or comment, and this guy has his hand up the whole hour! It's disrupting the class. I don't care what you have to do, just get him out of my class."

So I called him. "Dick," I said, "I want to start a new class—just you and me."

"What's it about?" he asked.

"It's about you and me becoming all God wants us to be." So while the pastor led the big class in the sanctuary, Dick and I met in the hall. I soon discovered why Dick demanded so much attention. He had some enormous needs and some serious personal problems. However, he also had a serious desire to follow Jesus. I couldn't have foreseen what Dick would become, but if I had had the eyes of Jesus, I would have spent more time preparing for our one-on-one class. No, he didn't become another Billy Graham, but he did develop into a solid disciple, married a lovely widow in the church, joined the choir, and for many years now has had a discipling ministry with men at the city rescue mission.

Lest you think it always turns out so well, let me give you the sequel to the story. Not long after Dick and I started our class, the senior pastor pointed out another disruptive fellow who needed to join our special class. The first week, Bob dominated the conversation. He talked non-stop. Finally Dick said, "Bob, you talk too much. I used to be like that. So here's what we're going to do . . ." Bob stayed with it for several weeks, and Dick and I came to love the guy. But when it came time to take some serious steps in following Jesus, Bob dropped out and we never saw him again. We experienced the same sadness Jesus felt when the rich young ruler wouldn't make a full commitment and walked away (Mark 10:17-31).

Remember that most of the first disciples were intimidated by the recently converted Saul of Tarsus. They wouldn't have anything to do with him. But Barnabas said, "Let me work with him" (see Acts 9:26-27), and he took Saul/Paul as a special project. For the next couple chapters of the Book of Acts, the team is described as Barnabas and Paul. Then a change takes place: it's now the Paul and Barnabas team. The disciple has surpassed his mentor in public leadership, and that's how it should be. After a while, Paul chose his own team, and Barnabas went looking for another "problem case"—which happened to be young John Mark, who had been kicked off Paul's team because he was a quitter.

Many of our conversations with our friends are unproductive because we don't have the right goal in view. We may be trying to help them overcome a particular problem, answer a troubling question, or resolve a pressing conflict. Those are temporary issues. We need to keep the ultimate goal in constant view. We need to see the current issue as one step toward the grand objective: Christlikeness.

Here's a suggestion: don't say "I'm discipling so-and-so." That implies a two-level relationship, as though you're the teacher, he or she is the student; you're the coach, he or she is the trainee; you're the counselor, he or she is the counselee; you're the mature believer, he or she is the baby Christian. All those statements may be true, but don't say them, because (1) it could wreck the relationship, and (2) he or she may soon surpass you in maturity and leadership. The goal is for you two friends to walk together as you follow Jesus. If you start off with a split-level relationship, you could get locked into that pattern and your friend's growth could be stunted.

The conversations we have with our friends take on eternal significance when we frame them in an eternal perspective. From the outset our friends need to know the reason we're meeting. We need to agree on the goal and repeat it often: to help each other become all God wants us to be to grow to full maturity in Christ.

One time I gathered a group of college guys together for a Bible study. We'd meet at a popular restaurant and discuss passages of Scripture. One day a mutual friend passed our table and asked, "What are you guys up to?" Before I could give a dignified answer, one of the college guys said, "Mike is helping us study the Bible, but we have no idea where he's headed with this. Maybe it's part of a course or something." What an indictment! I'd failed to give them the framework, and they hadn't bought into the goal because I hadn't given any.

The best way we can state our goal is, "John, I'd like to get together with you to help you become all God wants you to be. I can't say precisely what that is; you have to find that out for yourself. But I want to help you get there. All I ask in return is that you do the same for me. We're fellow strugglers in this pilgrimage of being and doing all God has for us." Then repeat that goal often as you meet.

## For Reflection and Discussion

1. What should be the goal of a disciple-making conversation?

2. Why shouldn't "salvation" be the goal?

3. What must a disciple-maker be able to see in a struggling new believer?

4. Why shouldn't you say, "I'm discipling John (or someone else)"?

# four

## elements

### of an

# Effective

## conversation

Conversations are the primary tool for making disciples; that's why they are so important. That tool is sharpened by understanding the difference between effective discussions and "just talk." If we want to see significant results from our interactions, we must pay the price of learning the skills of effective conversation.

If you were invited to an interview with the leader of your country, you would prepare in advance what you were going to say. You wouldn't think of engaging a world leader without adequate preparation. So, which is more important to God's eternal kingdom: a chat with the president or a breakfast conversation with your friend? The latter, of course, if you look at the situation from an eternal perspective.

Here are four elements that every effective conversation should contain:

1. A clear goal
2. Shared information that relates to that goal
3. Strengthening of the relationship
4. Agreement on the next steps toward the goal

First, let's start with the goal. The reason we engage in redemptive discussions with our friends is that both of us are committed to following Jesus. We want to be like Him and to do His will and work. Every time you meet with your friends, you need to keep that objective in mind. All parties to the conversation must agree that this is where the conversation is headed.

My wife, Martha, has done a great job decorating our home. From the earliest days of our marriage she has impressed on me that every detail of the home environment has a purpose. Some of the purposes of the home are functional, like arranging the laundry room for optimal utilization. Others relate to hospitality, and she is rewarded when visitors say, "I feel so comfortable in your home." The carefully arranged clusters of photos on our walls reinforce our family heritage; that's a purpose.

Our home also has a spiritual purpose: to help us be better disciples of Jesus Christ. So, on the wall over our dining room table is a framed needlework piece that artfully says, ". . . so we make it our goal to please him" (2 Cor. 5:9). Every time we sit down as a family for dinner and conversation, the goal is ever before us. There have been many times when the discussion at the table has strayed from that purpose, but the statement is there to pull us back to the goal.

So it should be when we talk with our friends. We should always ask, "What can we talk about today that will help us in our walk with Christ?" Or, "We're all determined to follow Jesus. What can we talk about today that will help us take the next steps?" Part of the prayer before we eat or talk or both should be, "Lord, help us see what You want us to do today."

One of my heroes was the Civil War chaplain and leader of the American Sunday School movement, Henry Clay Trumbull. He grew up in an amazing family, many of whose children, grandchildren, and great-grandchildren have had an enormous influence on the Church and significant institutions throughout the world. Every evening, his father, Gurdon Trumbull, would prepare questions and topics for dinner table discussion, while Mrs. Trumbull prepared the meal. Out of those powerful conversations grew the character qualities that prepared his children for leadership in public life. And they set an example for spiritual training that several generations of the Trumbull family followed.

Regarding this subject of conversations, in one of my classes a student objected to what he considered regimentation of discussions. "I just like to be free to talk about whatever comes up," he said. "I don't like to be bound by rules. I want to say whatever comes to my mind," to which I answered: "It's not all about you."

Lots of people want to talk, and they do. They drone on and on about whatever strikes their fancy. But self-centered conversations don't accomplish much. If we want to serve God first, others second, and ourselves last, we need to shape the direction of our discourse.

A few Sundays ago a friend and I visited another church. The preacher was obviously unprepared, and he offered a lame excuse about "I lost my notes on the way to church." Then he rambled on for 45 minutes. As we left the church, my friend snorted, "That guy blew a golden opportunity to affect the lives of 200 people. He wasted our time! He didn't have enough discipline to craft a message that would benefit all of us."

Yes, that's tragic. But how many times have we done

the same thing? How many golden opportunities have we had to invest in the lives of fellow believers and wasted them by talking about trivial issues? The touchstone that keeps us focused on eternal values is keeping the goal in mind.

Second, we share vital information—information that helps us get to the objective. When a salesman makes a presentation to a prospective buyer, he shares information that will help his client make a decision. What are the salient facts the prospect needs to know in order to purchase his product or service? If the information isn't relevant to the sale, he's just talking, not selling.

The content of a redemptive conversation depends on the level of maturity of the parties involved. The apostle John took this into consideration when he wrote to his friends (1 John 2:12-14). First he addresses those who were just beginning their walk with Christ: "I write to you, dear children, because your sins have been forgiven on account of his name" (v. 12). Those new believers just needed to be assured of their eternal life, to know that they were accepted in the family of God. That's the information spiritual children need to know.

Then he turns his attention to growing Christians: "I write to you, young men, because you have overcome the evil one" (v. 13), and "I write to you, young men, because you are strong, and the word of God lives in you, and you have overcome the evil one" (v. 14b). Why does he mention overcoming "the evil one" twice? Because that is a pri-

the

key

ingredient to

strengthening our

Relationships

is trust.

mary issue of struggling disciples: dealing with temptation, overcoming bad habits, correcting wrong behavior, and avoiding the pitfalls so common to youth.

Then John turns to the positive information to be shared: developing spiritual strength and building the Word of God into the fabric of life. This is the content of disciple-building conversations—how we can live our lives according to the principles of Scripture and what we can learn about spiritual strength.

Finally, John addresses mature Christians: "I write to you fathers, because you have known him who is from the beginning" (v. 14*a*). Knowing God better—that's the subject of discourse with senior saints. I've had the privilege of sitting in on conversations with great Christian leaders—men and women who lead large ministries and accomplish great things for the Kingdom. Do you know what they talk about? No, not the logistics of directing major enterprises or the problems that arise from dealing with difficult people. Almost always they talk about knowing God better and walking more closely with Him.

The most effective conversations share information before, during, and after the conversation itself. The people who make the most difference in other people's lives are constantly sending each other supplementary material: books, articles, quotations, personal notes, tapes, or reports. People who are good at this follow up their discussions with a note that reaffirms their discussion, perhaps with an enclosure—an article, a photo, or a news clipping.

And, just as often, they send some information prior to actually meeting: "John, you mentioned your interest in serving the poor in our own community. Here's an article on 'Neighborhood Networks' that might give you some ideas. We can discuss it when we meet on Tuesday."

The third goal for every effective conversation is that it strengthen the relationship. I visualize a friendship like a spider web: every interaction is one more gossamer strand that enhances the web. The strongest friendships are developed by working on meaningful projects, whether those projects are missions or personal pilgrimages. As we make progress together toward a noble goal, talking to each other along the way, a deep bond of commitment grows between us.

The key ingredient to strengthening our relationships is trust. That's what Jesus said is the basis for our friendship with Him: we trust Him to be who He said He is and to do what He said He would do (John 14:1). Trust is built by promises kept and experiences shared. Trust is destroyed by breaking confidences, pushing our own agenda, using the friendship for personal advantage, pushiness, and not following through. Once trust is lost, it is very difficult to regain.

Remember, the inner workings of your friend's soul is private territory. You enter there by invitation only. No matter how brilliant your observations may be concerning your friend's character and conduct, you must not share those insights until you have been given permission to do so.

Fourth and finally, an effective conversation ends with agreement on steps that need to be taken. Much of my own work deals with mentoring twenty-somethings—young men and women who are either students or fledgling professionals. I used to be amazed at the messes they could get themselves into, but I've come to realize that's the nature of the beast. They learn by doing and often by doing it wrong. When they're together, they're sometimes like a bunch of cats in a box: somebody always has his or her back up and claws out about something, whether it's a perceived threat or an injustice. Somebody else has his or her feelings hurt or pride offended. Then our conversations have to deal with dual issues: cleaning up the mess, then doing it right.

Paul wrote to his young friend Timothy about how to handle all these growth issues. In 2 Tim. 3:16 he writes, "All Scripture is God-breathed and is useful for teaching, rebuking, correcting and training in righteousness." That's a good formula for determining what steps need to be taken. Step 1: teaching—find the scriptural principle that addresses this particular problem. Step 2: rebuke—that is, point out what needs to change. Step 3: correcting—deciding what steps need to be taken to get back on track. Step 4: training in righteousness—building the positive disciplines that will keep the problem from happening again.

Some years ago I participated in a wonderful training

program for men in east Texas. A dozen or so men at a time would commit themselves to spend six weekends together, discussing the teachings of Jesus and deciding how to put them into practice. At the end of every weekend, each man made a list of the steps he intended to take before the next gathering. He chose an accountability partner who would call him regularly to check on his progress. Then he would give a report at the next session. The great growth that took place in these men's lives was not the outcome of their study, but the quality of the steps each one took.

Group discussion may produce enlightenment and intellectual stimulation, but it requires an action plan to accomplish spiritual growth and/or completion of a mission. One of the most helpful practices is visualizing spiritual achievement. It's helpful enough to spend a whole chapter on.

If you had a tool that didn't work, what would you do with it? Let's say your computer locks up or your saw won't cut; what's your solution? Either you fix it or replace it. In the same way, many of our conversations don't work. They're just wasted air. So let's fix them. Let's learn the principles of effective conversation and put them into practice. Then we'll see what God can do through friends who spur one another on to love and good works.

## For Reflection and Discussion

1. When you meet with your friend to talk about your walk with Christ, how would you state the goal or purpose of your conversation?

2. What is the advantage of having a clear and mutually agreed-upon goal for discussion?

3. How did the apostle Paul communicate his goal to the growing disciples in the Early Church?

4. On what basis should you discuss sensitive issues in your friend's life?

5. Review: What are the four elements of an effective conversation?

# ministering

# Out

## of the

# overflow

In the churches of my childhood the highest ambition of any Christian was to go into the ministry. If a young man or woman was totally committed to Christ, he or she went into the ministry. A local church was considered successful if several people went into the ministry from that congregation.

"The ministry" meant a professional career as a religious specialist. There was an unspoken hierarchy of valor even among those specialized careers. If you were committed to Christ, you became a pastor. If you were more committed, you became a traveling evangelist or Bible teacher. If you were totally sold out to Jesus, you became a foreign missionary. And at the top of the ladder was the highest calling: a medical missionary.

We grew up idolizing those heroes, like Dr. Albert Schweitzer, toiling alone in the jungles of Africa, nominated for the Nobel Peace Prize, and entertaining himself playing Bach on a mildewed organ in a thatched hut. Now that was going into the ministry!

Well, I was a hot-blooded young Christian, and I wanted to be all God wanted me to be, so I decided to go for the Holy Grail, the ultimate prize: I'd be a medical missionary. I felt quite good about that.

So I studied premed in college and was accepted into medical school. However, I had failed to be realistic about my own limitations: I didn't like working with sick people. I didn't have the temperament to be a doctor. Hospitals made me nauseous (and still do). If someone threw up, he or she had two problems: the mess on the floor and me on the floor.

So I retreated to a lower rung on the ladder of spiritual achievement—a fallback position: I went to seminary and became a traditional pastor. Bad choice! I didn't like preaching sermons any more than I liked working in smelly hospitals. I certainly didn't like calling on parishioners who were sick and needed pastoral comfort.

Somewhere along the line I made a wonderful discovery: ministry is not something you go into, it's something that comes out of you. It's the overflow of your walk with God. Yes, ministry is a high calling, but it is the calling of every Christian—not just the professional elite. A kindergarten teacher or a car salesman can have as profound a ministry as a pastor or missionary—even a medical missionary.

In the 15th chapter of John, Jesus used the word picture of a grapevine to illustrate our intimate relationship with Him. He is the Vine, the source of life. We are branches, receiving our spiritual vitality by abiding in Him. As long as we abide in the Vine, His life-giving Spirit nourishes our human spirits.

As we abide, an amazing process begins to take place: fruit appears. At first that fruit may seem like tiny blossoms, but those flowers soon become little buds and eventually clusters of fully developed fruit.

In Scripture, "fruit" has two meanings. The fruit of the Spirit, as described in Gal. 5:22, is Christian character: love, joy, peace, longsuffering, gentleness, patience, goodness, meekness, faith, and temperance. Those are the outward expressions of abiding in Christ. We can't produce them independently of fellowship with Him any more than a branch can produce grapes on its own. Fruit is merely the natural byproduct of abiding.

Fruit also is the reproductive seed of the gospel, just as the grape contains the seeds of future grapevines. This is the way the kingdom of God expands—the multiplication of fruit that occurs when branches abide in the Vine. Fruit is not an initiative planned by the branch. In the same way, spiritual fruit is the not the result of an organized church program. It is, like character, a natural consequence of abiding in the Vine. A Christian can no more say, "Look at the disciples I produced" than the branch can say, "Look at the grapes I produced." The life comes from the Vine, not the branch.

The mechanism for producing spiritual fruit is called ministering. The New Testament word for the verb "to minister" is *diakonein*. It's the Greek word from which we derive the term *deacon*. However, not only those who are appointed deacons are to be ministers. In fact, every normal Christian should be a minister. A minister displays the fruit of the Spirit in his or her character and bears the tangible fruit of "good works, which God prepared in advance for us to do" (Eph. 2:10).

A healthy branch produces fruit by ministering, which is simply to serve, to help, to assist. Spiritual energy is channeled from the Vine to the branches and on into the Church and the world through ministering. The term is general, but the applications are specific and widely varied. For example, in Acts 6:1-7, seven men are assigned to distribute food to the Greek widows. That was their ministry. The apostle Paul ministered by preaching the gospel to the Gentiles (2 Cor. 4:1), and the Corinthian church ministered by giving money to the struggling church in Jerusalem (9:1 ff.). Ministry always entails relationships, and relationships require communication. So, the way to improve your ministry is to improve your conversations.

A great transformation is taking place in the Church around the world today. I call it the Third Great Reformation. The first reformation (the Protestant Reformation) took place in the 16th century when leaders like Martin Luther and others translated the Bible into the language of the people and made it widely available. The second reformation (the Evangelical Awakening) took place in the 18th century under the leadership of John Wesley, John Whitefield, and others. That transformation returned Christian living to the heart, not just doctrinal propositions. Today's reformation is putting the ministry back into the hands of all believers, not just those who are ordained as professional clergy.

One key passage relevant to this sea change is Eph. 4, where the role of Christian leaders is defined as "equipping of the saints for the work of ministry" (v. 12, NKJV). The job of apostles, prophets, evangelists, pastors, and

teachers is not to do the ministry but to equip every follower of Jesus to bear fruit by ministering to others. We do
that by allowing what God is doing in our own lives to
spill over, to overflow, into the lives of others.

Here's an example: Last Saturday, I was having a cup
of coffee in the local bookstore. I noticed a man sitting by
himself, so I introduced myself and sat down. Within a few
minutes I learned that my friend's name was Chuck. He's a
Seventh-Day Adventist, and he's a naturalist. He is writing
a children's book on bears. Chuck knows all about bears,
probably more than most bears know, and he shared lots
of interesting facts with me about their habits. He also got
to know something about me, about my personal walk
with Christ, and about the issues I am currently wrestling
with. Before the hour was up, Chuck was ministering to
me. Out of the overflow of his own healthy friendship
with Christ, he encouraged me and strengthened my faith
in God's provision. Before I left, Chuck prayed with me
(with everyone in the coffee shop looking on) and sent
me on my way with a blessing.

On the negative side, Jesus gave a stern warning
about failure to bear fruit. He assumed that if it isn't bear-
ing fruit, the branch is dead. The problem is not a lack of
effort on the part of the branch to bear fruit; it is a failure
to abide in the Vine.

In a certain sense, failure to bear fruit is a good thing.
It can be an indicator of poor spiritual health in the
branch. Just as pain serves a useful function in maintaining

physical health, so fruitlessness serves a useful function in our spiritual lives. It indicates that there is a disconnect between the Vine and the branch. It is a warning to check the Vine-to-branch relationship.

I have found that it is possible for someone to preach great sermons, teach a Bible class, or sing beautiful Christian music without abiding in the Vine. However, it is impossible to bear fruit in that condition. A talented orator may preach a great message without having an intimate communion with Christ. However, he or she cannot bear fruit in a one-to-one ministry of helping another person follow Jesus. It's impossible to make disciples when your soul is running on empty.

How can I make such a strong statement? Because I've been there many times. I've sat across the table from men who are eager to take the next step in following Jesus, and I've experienced that sickening feeling of having nothing to offer them. There's nothing more pitiful than an empty cup trying to overflow. I know; I've tried it.

The best crucible in which to test our relationship with the Vine is one-to-one conversation with a fellow struggler. If we can't minister to him or her out of the abundance of our own walk with Christ, then it should drive us to our knees to repair the Vine-to-branch connection. Our first priority as branches is not to produce fruit; it is to abide in the Vine.

Jesus said, "Out of the abundance of the heart the mouth speaks" (Matt. 12:34, NKJV). Making disciples is a heart-to-heart enterprise. Singing to an audience or preaching to a crowd is a mouth-to-ear transaction and can be done (although it shouldn't be) without ministering out of the overflow. But making disciples requires a full heart.

It was my privilege to serve on a church staff with a man who was an expert in personal evangelism. Week after week he led his team of trainees out into the community to follow up with those who had filled out a visitor's card the previous Sunday. As his team called on visitors in their homes, some of those people were ready to make sincere commitments to follow Jesus. However, most of the time people didn't respond.

So I asked him, "Joe, why do you keep your team calling on visitors when the results are so poor and the work is so discouraging?"

His answer has proven very useful to me in the ensuing years: "My main task is bringing my team members to maturity in Christ. Presenting the gospel to unbelievers is just the laboratory in which the discipling process can be guided and developed. Just like Jesus took His men through the towns and villages to teach them the principles of the Kingdom, so I'm taking my guys into the neighborhoods primarily for their sake, not primarily for the task of evangelism. If they are engaged every week in confronting the powers of darkness with the light of the gospel, it keeps them from getting footsy with the world."

The apostle Paul set this high standard for personal ministry: "You follow me as I follow Christ" (1 Cor. 11:1, author's paraphrase). The secret to a more fruitful ministry is not learning slick, packaged presentation techniques. The key is following Jesus more closely. We improve our work by improving our walk. As we walk in fellowship with Him, enjoying His presence and obeying His commands, we place ourselves in a position others will want to follow.

The great East Africa Revival that started in Rwanda in the 1920s and spread throughout much of east-central Africa is still being felt today. One of the hallmarks of that revival was the practice called *walking in the light,* by which they meant "instant confession; instant obedience." The great African saints at the core of that movement did not have to conjure up a ministry: it flowed from them as they walked in the light. They had such an intimate communion with Christ that whole communities were transformed by their witness. Abiding in the Vine produced a great harvest of fruit. The secret was not a churchwide fruit-bearing campaign or a denominational program; it was abiding in the Vine.

Every new generation has to relearn the ancient truth: God's kingdom spreads throughout the world through personal relationships. The *sap* of the gospel flows from the Vine to the branches and overflows into the surrounding world through its fruit. Those branches who abide in the Vine produce more branches through their self-sacrificing ministry to one friend at a time, one conversation at a time.

## For Reflection and Discussion

1. What happens when we "abide in the Vine"?

2. What is the source of effective ministry?

3. In what sense could there be a positive value in the failure to bear fruit in personal ministry?

4. What is the Third Reformation that is taking place in the Church today?

six

john

# Wesley's "close conversations"

John Wesley was an 18th-century preacher whose ministry revolutionized England—spiritually, morally, politically, and economically. The driving force of this national transformation was not Wesley's talent or personality, it was the transforming power of God's Holy Spirit. Mr. Wesley simply developed the tools to harness that power. His secret was to guide new Christian believers through the steps of personal spiritual growth, one structured conversation at a time. He developed a network of small groups by which the poor, the illiterate, and the uneducated could develop Christian character and be equipped with the tools to change society through the power of the Holy Spirit.

Wesley had a great advantage: he built on a strong biblical theology. He built a system to accomplish the goal he believed was the ultimate purpose of God: to produce Christlikeness, having the mind of Christ and doing the work of God in the world. He called it "spreading scriptural holiness throughout the land." He started with the right goal, then experimented until he found the right methods to enable people to get to the goal.

The setting for the Wesleyan revolution was a demographic upheaval very similar to the chaotic urbanization taking place in third world countries today. Waves of poor and uneducated people flocked to the newly industrialized cities of London, Liverpool, Newcastle, and Birmingham, just as they are flocking to Lagos and Delhi and Mexico City today. They left behind the relative stability of the village and crowded into wretched urban slums, hoping for a better life. What they got instead was grinding poverty, violence, exploitation, and disease. They succumbed to vices unknown in their feudal hamlets: alcoholism, prostitution, smuggling, gambling, and thievery.

The living conditions were deplorable: sewage ran through the streets, enabling diseases to spread in epidemic waves. Children were forced to work in bleak factories and brickyards, often as young as three and four years old. There was no police protection, fire control, or medical care. Worst of all there was no spiritual or moral instruction. Religious services were legally restricted to official church buildings, none of which were located in the impoverished ghettos. Clergymen seldom ventured into the townships, since their salaries were paid by wealthy parishioners.

The slums were so wretched that it was unsafe to enter them without an armed guard. However, as in every dark period of human history, God raised up a band of spiritual leaders. John Wesley was not the only preacher, or even the best, who proclaimed the gospel to England's poor, but he was the one who perfected a method that could channel their newfound faith into practical growth.

Wesley had spiritual vision: he looked at the same mess everybody else looked at but saw what few others could see—a great opportunity for the kingdom of God. He looked at those slum dwellers and saw what God could do in and through them. He was realistic about their terrible condition but hopeful about their potential. He saw them through the eyes of Jesus.

Here's his journal entry as he entered one of the slums around Newcastle:

> We came to Newcastle about six, and, after a short refreshment, walked into the town. I was surprised: so much drunkenness, cursing, and swearing (even from the mouths of little children) do I never remember to have seen or heard before, in so small a compass of time. Surely this place is ripe for Him who "came not to call the righteous, but sinners to repentance."

> At seven I walked down to Sandgate, the poorest and most contemptible part of the town, and, standing at the end of the street with John Taylor, began to sing the hundredth Psalm. Three or four people came out to see what was the matter, who soon increased to four or five hundred. I suppose there might be twelve to fifteen hundred before I had done preaching.*

Those who responded to his public preaching, as here at Newcastle, Wesley gathered into small groups called class meetings. A leader from that community was appointed to give oversight to each group, and Wesley se-

---

*Quoted in Martin Schmidt, *John Wesley: A Theological Biography,* 2 volumes, tr. Norman P. Goldhawk (London: The Epworth Press, 1962), 2:72-73.

cured their commitment to a rigid set of rules—not rules for conduct or theology or church membership, but guidelines for redemptive conversations. Through trial and error, he had formulated an instructional method, which, if followed consistently, would transform raw converts into mature Christians. He was so insistent on maintaining those methods, his followers were derisively called Methodists.

Every week these struggling new Christians met in groups of 6 to 12 to talk about their spiritual progress or lack of it. They talked. They engaged in guided conversations. They "confess[ed their] faults one to another" (James 5:16, KJV) as was the practice of the Early Church. They encouraged each other to spiritual growth in the context of intimate personal friendships. And those discussions brought about a national revival.

Here's how the discussions went every week: the leader (not a professional clergyman) first gave his answers to a prescribed set of questions. They were formulated in the quaint terminology of the 18th century but are just as relevant to spiritual growth today. The first question was: "How doth your soul prosper?" Here the leader described his personal walk with Christ that week. Second was, "What advantage have you taken of the means of grace?" In other words, what are you doing to foster your own spiritual growth—attending church services, family prayers, reading the Bible, reading good books, and so forth? Third: "What opportunities have you had for service and witness and how did you avail yourself of them?" Last-

people

are

discovering

the power

of close

conversations.

ly: "What temptations have you faced and how did you overcome them?" Then each member of the group answered the same questions, one at a time.

In the context of a loving, supporting fellowship, people talked about the reality of following Jesus. They shared their victories and defeats. They encouraged each other. They prayed for each other. They "stimulate[d] one other to love and good deeds" (Heb. 10:24, NASB) as prescribed in Scripture. And as they grew, England was transformed. Hundreds of thousands of coal miners and factory workers were converted, their families were strengthened morally and spiritually, and their communities were transformed. Through the power of small groups the poor were given the tools for economic advancement, the illiterate were educated, the sick were treated, and the whole nation lifted morally and socially.

There was no teaching, no preaching, no training given in the class meetings. People just talked about their personal lives, and God's Holy Spirit performed the miracle of personal transformation. As people were changed, one conversation at a time, the society was changed—from the bottom up.

John Wesley recognized powerful conversations as the indispensable key to spiritual growth. He called the personal interviews he conducted with those early Methodists "close conversation." What a beautiful term for intimate, productive discussion! On one occasion he wrote, "I have found by experience that one of those [people] has learned more from one hour's close discourse than ten years' public preaching!"

A refreshing revival is beginning to take place in many places throughout the Christian world: people are discovering the power of close conversations. Stagnant congregations and dying denominations are realizing that traditional public worship services are insufficient to bring people to maturity in Christ. Public preaching and congregational programs are not effective vehicles to bring about personal renewal on the scale of the Wesleyan revolution. The new method that is transforming churches and communities is the technique John Wesley applied in the 18th century: intimate discussions. Wesley himself did not claim to be inventing something new but was merely rediscovering the standard practices of the 1st-century Church.

## For Reflection and Discussion

1. How did John Wesley express the goal of his movement?

2. What was the secret of his success in leading the nation of England to spiritual transformation?

3. What was Wesley's target audience?

4. What new methods did he employ?

seven

# Focus

## on the

# faithful

Most religious programs target the wrong people. They concentrate on those who are interested enough in Christian issues to come to church or attend a program but who are not committed enough to take serious steps to follow Jesus. Week after week those uncommitted listeners hear the same challenges until they become immune to the stirrings of conscience. They are like the crowds who followed Jesus. They liked to see the signs and wonders, but they stayed home when He started talking about risky commitments.

However, there were a few who continued to follow Him. Every time He turned around, they were right there at His elbow, asking questions and making immature attempts to do what He asked them to do. Those were the ones He invested His life in. He was modeling for His disciples and for us an important principle: focus on those who are faithful.

This principle was made practical to me through a little book by Gene Warr titled *You Can Make Disciples*. He said we should look at every religious gathering as a fishing pond for faithful people. Don't chase the spectators away, just find the doers among them and give special attention to those. For example, he taught a Sunday School class at his church. All the people who attended were nice, pleasant people who wouldn't be there at all if they didn't have some level of Christian commitment. However, he found his faithful few by giving a simple assignment at the end of each lesson. The next week, he'd see who did it, or at least tried. Then he'd meet them outside class for coffee or lunch and have a serious conversation about taking the next steps in following Jesus. He invested in those men, to great spiritual profit.

So, I've tried to do the same. One time, I was having lunch at a truck stop in Greenfield, Indiana. Two fellows, whom I recognized as regular customers, were having a loud and heated argument about religion. One of them, looking for support, came over to my table. "You must be religious," he said, "because we saw you bow your head before you had lunch. Tell us which one is right!" I didn't want to take sides, but I saw an opportunity. So, I said, "Come next Thursday and I'll give you an answer." I set a time in the future for several reasons: one, I wanted to direct the discussion on my terms, not in terms of their argument. Two, I wanted some time for their passions to cool down. But mostly, I wanted time to look up the answers. "And," I said, "bring some of your friends with you."

The next week we had an enjoyable discussion, based in Scripture, that was somewhat close to what they had been arguing about. They all seemed to enjoy the give-and-take of a conversation centered around the Bible, not just pooled ignorance. We continued to meet, week after week, until our group outgrew the restaurant. So we moved out to Mac's Steak House at the junction of Route 9 and Interstate 70. The steak house had a big enough parking lot to handle big rigs off the highway, and an hour before every gathering our guys would get on the CB and invite over-the-road truckers to join us. Quite a few did, and our group soon swelled to 30 or 40 men.

However, I wasn't looking for a crowd. I was looking for a few faithful men. So every week I'd give a simple assignment: "OK, we've read today that husbands should love their wives as Christ loved the Church. What I want you to do this week is to tell your wife every day, in some way or another, that you love her, and do one nice thing for her every day." That brought some interesting responses. One guy said, "My wife thinks I'm up to something. She's suspicious that I'm covering something up." Everybody laughed. A couple others indicated they had at least tried to complete the assignment. And I had found my faithful men. I built friendships with them outside the group—friendships that could lead to spiritual depth. Some of those men are friends of mine to this day, and they're walking with the Lord in obedience to His Word. Everybody had a nice time, but a few became real disciples.

I've met a lot of resistance to this principle of concentrating on a few faithful people, especially from pastors. They tell me, "I have to treat all my parishioners the same, or else some will think I'm showing favoritism." My response is, "My, you're more spiritual than Jesus, because that's what He did." Many of those who objected to this idea have come back years later with great sadness. "I invested years of my life with those people, and they let me down. When it came time to take the hard steps, they bailed out." To which I reply, "You chose the wrong people in the first place. You wasted your time on people who weren't committed to following through. There's no greater waste of your life than investing in a person who isn't faithful."

As Jesus so often said to His friends, the key issue is not what a person says but whether he or she does the will of God. He summed up His Sermon on the Mount with the story of two builders—one wise, one foolish. The wise man built on the rock of Jesus' teachings, and his house stood the test of storms. The foolish man built on the sand, and his house was swept away. So, what was the sand on which the foolish man built? It might have been the teachings of Jesus! At least that's what Jesus said: "The foolish man hears my word . . ." His foolishness was not a matter of ignorance; it was simply failure to act on what he knew to be true. He may have agreed completely with what Jesus said. He could even have taught a class on "The Teachings of Jesus" and conveyed them accurately to his students. But he was foolish because he didn't put them into practice. The man Jesus is looking for is the doer. May we follow His example.

The apostle James gave the same advice to early Christians: "Be doers of the word, and not hearers only, deceiving yourselves" (1:22, NKJV). People who hear the truth but fail to put it into practice fall into the self-delusion of spiritual complacency. They think they are well off spiritually because they come, listen, agree with everything the pastor preaches, and do their share of duties around the church. But their spiritual life has no depth because they are "hearers only."

I've just recently lost a great friend, a man who died in the prime of life in a boating accident. I spent hundreds of hours with him, talking about lots of matters of mutual interest, but also talking about the Lord. We'd meet at Acapulco Joe's for Mexican food, talk about the kids and politics and boats and Jesus. We were ruthlessly honest with each other, confessing our failures and celebrating even the smallest successes. The reason I felt good about my investment is that he was a doer of the Word. If he came to the conclusion that Jesus was instructing him, through the Bible, to make changes in his life or business, he would do so even at great personal cost or risk. I jumped on that. He was a faithful man and a wise investment of my time. And, to my delight, I discovered that I was an equal or greater beneficiary of our friendship since he also challenged me to take steps of my own.

When you find a friend who is faithful in following Jesus, you've discovered a gold mine. If you can help him or her take the next steps in spiritual growth, you will have made the finest investment a person can make in this life.

I read an interesting story from the life of Dawson Trotman, founder of the Navigators and one of America's finest producers of Christian leaders. He talked to his associate, Lorne Sanny, about transferring Sanny to another city where there was opportunity to start a new ministry.

As they assessed the situation, Trotman asked Sanny, "How's your current ministry going?"

"Well, we have some Bible studies going and a few men are responding pretty well."

"Do you have any men who are really faithful, genuinely serious about following Jesus?" Trotman asked.

"I do have one fellow. He's kinda rough, a cowboy type, but he is definitely a faithful man. His name is Charlie Riggs."

"Well," said Trotman, "you'd better stay where you are. If you have one faithful man, you have a valuable asset."

Charlie Riggs turned out to be one of the most productive disciple-makers of our time, head of the Billy Graham follow-up team for several decades.

In your circle of friends there is surely one person who will follow Jesus faithfully. When you locate that man or woman, you have found the base for building a successful and long-lasting ministry. Pour your life into that one, regardless of his or her talents, abilities, charm, intelligence, or lack of all those things. The quality God is looking for is faithfulness, and He will build His kingdom through the influence of those people.

## For Reflection and Discussion

1. Who were the people Jesus invested His life in, and how did He choose them?

2. What qualities should we look for in a potential disciple, and how can we identify those qualities?

3. How did Jesus separate the faithful few from the crowd?

4. What can we expect if we invest in people who are not "doers of the word"?

eight

one

# good

question

is Worth a

thousand

# answers

Jesus was the model communicator. He chose 12 unlettered Galileans, mostly fishermen, and trained them to change the world. It took Him only three years to equip His friends to do God's will in their personal lives and God's work in the world. How did He do that? By effective conversations, usually employing strategic questions.

Good questions are shovels to dig down to reality, to truth, to the actual situation. Jesus' mission was to connect the eternal purpose of God with the reality of people's sinful condition, not only to announce God's plan but to enable its accomplishment in our lives. He used a human word picture to describe the plan of God; he called it the kingdom of God or the kingdom of heaven. God's kingdom is where the rule of God meets the reality of human life, and human life submits. Jesus said that's where the kingdom of God really is: in the hearts of people (Luke 17:21).

Resistance to the way of God's kingdom is called sin. Sin starts as just an idea, then eventually expresses itself in misconduct. Lust, greed, envy, hatred, pride, and bitterness all begin their existence as fantasies played out in the mind. Every thought or idea of a wrong action is an opportunity for sin to take hold. When perverted mental images are acted out in inappropriate or illegal ways it is the job of the judge and the policeman to deal with them. But dealing with the thoughts and intentions of the heart is the work of the Word of God by the Spirit of God. That's where Kingdom issues are settled. The purpose of disciple-building conversations is to help our friends come to grips with reality—the truth of God's Word and the truth of their own condition.

Jesus used questions to probe reality, to get to the core issues. "Who do men say that I am?" He asked (Mark 8:27, NKJV). "But who do you say that I am?" (v. 29, NKJV). The answers to those pivotal questions were the rocks on which He would build His Church. Before He could proceed with the training of the leaders of that Church, He had to make sure the foundational belief was firmly established in His disciples' minds. He determined that by asking penetrating questions.

As we follow His example, we should ask our friends questions that will help them deal with Kingdom issues. What is important in our conversations is not what we say or think but what our friends say and think about their walks with Christ. The critical belief in these conversations is not who I think Jesus is but who they think Jesus is. Good questions enable us to penetrate the surface façade and get down to the serious business of following Jesus.

Productive conversations start and end with productive questions. The first words of a verbal encounter set the stage for the rest of the interaction. "John, I'm glad we have this time to talk. I know you're serious about following Jesus, and I know your time is valuable. Let's make the most of it. What is the most important issue we can discuss today?" Or, you might ask, "What's on the growing edge of your relationship with Christ?" or "Is there a particular decision you need to make or an issue you need to clarify?" You should also ask, "Is there something you sense I should be tackling?" That insures that the conversation will be mutually beneficial—a discussion between fellow strugglers.

Here's an experience I know you've had: you've just come through a painful experience and you want to tell somebody about it. You begin to share with your friend but before you get the whole story on the table, your friend says, "I know exactly how you feel. I've had the same problem . . ." He or she grabs the conversation and runs with it. Your eyes begin to glaze over and mentally you begin to check out. You didn't initiate this conversation to hear his or her story—you wanted to tell yours. So you say, "How nice!" and walk away with the pain still throbbing in your heart.

Good questions take the focus off yourself. Instead, they define and clarify what God wants of each of us and how we relate to His desires. As you will recall from your reading of the third chapter of Genesis, God's relationship with our first parents, Adam and Eve, began with four questions about their relationship: "Where are you? . . . Who told you [this]? . . . Have you eaten from the tree that I commanded you not to eat from? . . . What is this you have done?" (vv. 9, 11*a,* 11*b,* 13).

As we and our friends seek to be God's people, the questions still fall into those same categories: Where are you spiritually? Are you doing or not doing what God asked you do to? Where did you get your information and is it correct? What are you going to do? At various times in our relationship the spotlight of God's truth will focus on one person, at other times on another, but at all times on what God intends. It is His intention to draw us to himself and teach us His ways. He is the Teacher; we are the learners.

It's so tempting to jump into redemptive discussions with your own wisdom, your own experience, your own intellectual solution. Don't! Bite your tongue and listen. If you're talking, you're not listening; if you're not listening, you're not learning; and if you're not learning, you're not making a disciple. You're just talking.

Good questions ask permission to delve into sensitive issues. If you don't have permission, don't go there. So ask, "Would you like to discuss _____ ?" If an issue is so pressing and so urgent that it needs addressing right now, and if your friend is avoiding the problem, ask, "How straight can you take it?" If he or she opens the door to that situation, then you may proceed carefully.

Good questions follow the crumbs back to the source of the problem. They peel off the outer layers of excuses and rationalization until the core issue is revealed.

Early in our child-rearing experience, Martha and I learned that good child discipline begins with appropriate questions. Don't ask a disobedient child, "Why did you do that?" That just trains a child to be an excuse-maker. Instead, the child needs to be trained to make right choices. A better question is, "What did you do?" And, "Was that the right way to handle the situation?" "How should you have dealt with this?" "What did you do to help create the problem?"

To maximize the potential of a conversation, start with introductory questions, proceed to issues that have a likelihood of spiritual progress, ask for permission to discuss them, and work toward practical steps of application. Here are some good questions to ask a friend who's struggling with a decision:

- What are your options?
- Who and what will be affected if this is not resolved?
- What is the ideal outcome? Describe the best-case scenario.
- What's keeping you from making this decision?
- How does this square with what Jesus said to do?
- What's at stake in this issue?
- What are the possible unintended consequences of each option?

I spent many profitable Tuesday breakfasts with my wise friend Mike DuKate. He was a master of helpful questions. One time he asked me, "What would happen if you just did what you know is right in this situation?"

I said, "I'd be absolutely humiliated. I'd be embarrassed to death!"

"Is that all that's holding you back?" he asked.

When I nodded yes, he said loudly enough for everybody at the next tables to hear, "You mean you're making a major decision on the basis of your silly pride?"

That was the tipping point. He had helped me make the right decision by asking the right questions. I saw clearly what was holding me back, and I made the commitment right then and there to act.

Good questions also keep our relationships with our friends in good working order. We need to use them to keep our friendships fresh and open. Jesus did this with His disciples—"Jesus said to the twelve, 'Do you also want to go away?' Then Simon Peter answered Him, 'Lord, to whom shall we go? You have the words of eternal life'" (John 6:67-68, NKJV).

I was fortunate to serve on a church staff with Ann Beattie, an effective trainer and mentor for church workers. One day she walked into my office and asked, "How would you like for me to tell you I'm so mad at you I could rip your lips off?"

I was taken aback: "What in the world have I done?"

"Nothing yet," she replied, "but sooner or later we're going to butt heads on some issue or another and we'll get very upset with each other. I just want to know how you want to handle it." It took me just a minute to give her my rules for a good clean fight:

1. Stick to the problem at hand; don't attack my character.
2. Don't allow a difference of opinion to ruin our friendship.
3. Don't embarrass me in public. Let's iron it out privately.

"OK," she said. "Where should we do that?"

"Down in the coffee shop," I suggested.

We got along for some years with no major conflict. Then one day a contentious issue came up in staff meeting. I stated my opinion, and Ann glared at me across the table and began to scribble a note. She passed it around the table, and I was sure everybody read it as it went by. "You're getting dangerously close to a coffee break!" it read. So I backed off, we hashed it out over coffee, and we went back to work with the issue resolved and our relationship intact.

Part of my heritage is in the Friends (Quaker) tradition. The Friends have a healthy tradition called the queries, a series of questions about personal and corporate life. Once a quarter, the clerk of the meeting reads the queries slowly, as the congregation sits in silence, allowing the Holy Spirit to convict or affirm our worship, conduct, and Christian service.

One of the best Quaker questions, often used to end a time of worship and fellowship, is "Are all hearts free?" I like to ask that at the conclusion of a session with my friend, just to make sure there are no dangling concerns, no loose ends.

Another important set of questions has to do with next steps. "What are you going to do about this?" "How can I help you do what you've said needs to be done?" "Should I call later this week to see how this worked out?"

Don't rescue your friends from their distress. That

don't

rescue your

Friends

from their

distress.

won't help them, and you have enough problems of your own. It doesn't make your friends strong to bail them out when they are facing a critical step. Let them make the decision. If you tackle the issue, and it fails, then you get the blame. If you succeed, your friends may be off the hook but they didn't learn anything in the process.

The kingdom of God is where human hearts meet the reality of God and bow in submission. The way to help your friends is to model that submission and help them do the same. The prayer God is waiting to hear from you and your friends is "Not my will, but thine, be done" (Luke 22:42, KJV). Good questions enable friends to engage in productive conversations, and productive conversations provide the foundation for doing the will of God. And doing the will of God is what the Kingdom is all about.

## For Reflection and Discussion

1. What were some of the questions Jesus used to get to the heart of an issue?

2. What are some questions that could reveal the state of your friend's spiritual journey?

3. When a friend is struggling with a difficult decision, what are some appropriate questions to ask?

4. If your friend is faced with a tough decision, why is it best not to rescue him or her?

nine

could

you not

Pray

with me?

Jesus' closest friends failed Him in His darkest hour. While He struggled in agony in the Garden of Gethsemane, they slept. He was wrestling with the most difficult issue for any child of God: my will or God's will? But His friends were too tired to help.

In one sense Jesus' prayer in Gethsemane was a once-in-history event, a cosmic turning point that will never be repeated. But in another sense, He was modeling for us what it means to surrender our will to God's will—a choice that we must make every day, sometimes many times a day. That choice is best made in the company of friends.

The Christian life is a group project, not a solitary quest. The optimal environment for doing God's will is a circle of friends who will pray us through those hard periods of spiritual struggle. John Wesley, whose methods for making disciples we'll discuss in another chapter, said, "All holiness is social holiness," by which he meant we are only able to live a holy life in interaction with other believers.

Spiritual growth is the process of replacing our natural human way of doing things with God's way. That process has some crisis points, as in when we are initially born into God's family or when we come to a point of total surrender to His will, but it is also a daily discipline. It is the transformation brought about by the Holy Spirit, at times in momentous leaps, at other times in tiny, painful steps. That process takes place best in the company of

could you not Pray with me?

thank God

for people

who won't

let us go

backward.

prayerful friends, friends who love us enough to keep us from turning back to the old way.

Early in my ministry I served on the staff of a church in Tulsa. Soon after I began working there, an older man in the church, a painting contractor, invited me to lunch. He had lots of questions, personal questions. "How are you getting along in your work? How's your prayer life? Are you struggling with any personal issues: temptations, resentments, frustrations, disappointments?" Every few weeks, he would take me to lunch and ask the same questions. Finally, I told him, "I enjoy meeting with you, but I'm not sure what you are trying to accomplish."

"I see part of my ministry," he said, "as supporting my pastors. I'm not an educated person, I haven't been to Bible school or seminary, and I don't presume that I can teach you anything about how to do your work. However, I see my role as the same as those spikes in the bank parking lot that let you drive forward but blow your tires out if you back up. I can't lead you forward, but I want to make sure you don't back up." Thank God for people who won't let us go backward.

I've read the biographies of great saints who seemed to make it on their own, who seemed to have everything they needed within themselves to follow Jesus successfully. I don't buy it. I've done my wilderness thing and made no progress at all. Left to myself, I gave in to powerful rationalizations for my poor performance and selfish indulgence. I discovered how brilliantly creative I could be in making excuses and dodging hard commitments. I need friends who can pray or "keep watch with me for one hour" (Matt. 26:40), just like Jesus did.

The spiritual life is a battle, a constant struggle with the desires of the flesh and the temptations of the Evil One. Our Heavenly Father designed us with the need to conquer self-will through the power of community—that network of friends who encourage us. None of us has the ability to make it on our own. That's the beauty of the Body of Christ: we need each other collectively to be all God wants us to be individually.

The kingdom of God is that realm where God's will is done, "on earth as it is in heaven" (Matt. 6:10). Membership in that Kingdom is not a transaction, it is a transformation. It is the replacement of our sinful nature with the character of Jesus himself. That's a lifelong process that requires divine enablement (grace) and corporate encouragement.

In their eagerness to promote the gospel, many salesmen for the Kingdom have reduced the Christian life to a mere transaction: "Just raise your hand and you'll have eternal life." Can you imagine Jesus saying to the multitudes, "Just fill out this card and your name will be written in the Lamb's Book of Life"? No way. When He said, "If you want to follow me, you have to be willing to die on a cross" (see Matt. 16:24-25), 95 percent of His hearers left. Only a few became genuine followers. The rest got all they wanted: a free fish sandwich, a good sermon, and the chance to see a few miracles.

Early in our marriage Martha and I met with two other couples for Bible study and prayer. Week after week, with no prearrangement, the spotlight seemed to focus on one couple or another who were going through difficult times of growth. One night, our problems came up. The big issue that always caused us conflict surfaced. It was that problem we never wanted to talk about but was the first thing that came up whenever we had a fight. We talked and prayed for hours, with no resolution. Finally, it was time to go home. The kids were tired, and we had to get them to bed. We left with no deliverance from our thorn in the flesh.

I dropped Martha and the kids off at home and went for a ride, indulging in the "pity poor mes" and blaming her for the unresolved conflict. After I'd rehearsed my excuses for nearly an hour, I drove home. I was astonished to find the other four members of our group waiting for me in our living room. "We knew you hadn't worked through to a successful conclusion," they said, "so we hired a babysitter to stay with our kids and we're going to stay here and pray with you until you get it resolved." Wow! What friends! Once we saw there was no backing out, we tackled the problem head-on and soon worked our way through the logjam.

Prayer together is the foundation of redemptive friendships. There are many types of productive discussions between friends, but without prayer those are just more self-help mechanisms. When you pray with your friend, you invite a divine partner to your project. The Holy Spirit enables the kind of transformation you have been wishing for, both in the life of your friend and in your own.

So, the central question on which your conversations should be built is, "What can I pray with you about?" Especially if your friend is a new Christian, he or she is unlikely to ask for prayer for any deep, significant struggle. You have to prove yourself faithful to pray. When you do actually intercede as requested, and ask next time you meet, "How's it going with your problem at work?" or "What's happening with the mortgage issue we prayed about last week?" your prayer partner will have reason to trust you with more substantial spiritual concerns.

Remember, your friend's greatest need is not your attention or good advice. What he or she really needs is the power of God's Spirit to apply the truth of God's Word to the core issues of life. Great friendships are not built around great friends; they're built around a great God. Prayer connects people who love each other with the ultimate source of enablement and empowerment.

Augustine Davies from Sierra Leone is one of my prayer colleagues. He shared with me how he learned to pray. One of his professors at Africa Bible College asked him, "Gus, would you like to learn to pray? OK, then meet me every morning under this tree, and we'll pray from

6:00 until breakfast." So every morning they prayed, the prayer mentor with the eager student. It wasn't easy at first, Gus says, but he soon got in the rhythm of regular, habitual prayer. For many years now, that teacher's investment has paid rich dividends. Gus has led many people to faith in Christ and many new believers to mature faith by asking, "Would you like to learn to pray? OK, let's meet and pray."

You may not be a great Bible scholar or a gifted public speaker. You may not be able to engage in clever repartee or scintillating conversation. You may not have the experience to offer profound counsel. But you can pray. And your prayers with your friend will accomplish more in his or her life than any lectures, books, or sermons. Jesus taught His disciples to pray, and on that foundation He built a team that turned their world upside down.

## For Reflection and Discussion

1. How is Jesus' prayer in the Garden of Gethsemane the central prayer of Christian discipleship?

2. What is the value of friends praying together?

3. How did Jesus teach His disciples to pray?

4. How would you define "the kingdom of God"?

ten

the

word of

God vs.

your humble

opinion

This may come as a shock to you, but nowhere in Scripture has God promised to bless your humble opinion. He has, however, given every assurance that His Word will bring about significant changes when applied to the lives of people, specifically you and your friends. The value of Scripture in helping your friends follow Jesus (making disciples) is that it not only addresses the cognitive aspects of an issue, like forgiveness for example, but the emotional, social, and behavioral sides as well. As promised, "The word of God is . . . sharper than any two-edged sword, piercing even to the division of soul and spirit . . . and is a discerner of the thoughts and intents of the heart" (Heb. 4:12, NKJV).

Is your friend, the one you are helping become a disciple, struggling with a troublesome hurdle that he or she just can't seem to get over? Are you rummaging around in your college psychology notes or following leads on the Internet looking for an answer? Don't give in to the temptation to pull a rabbit out of the hat and come up with a brilliant solution to your friend's dilemma. There is a solution in God's Word that is better than any you can find among your own resources, and it comes with a guarantee.

The very purpose of Scripture is to accomplish exactly what you desire in your friend: Christlikeness in character and in practice. Analyze this statement from the apostle Paul, given to his apprentice Timothy: "All Scripture is given by inspiration of God [that's the authority], and is profitable for doctrine, for reproof, for correction, for instruction in righteousness [the various uses], that the man of

God may be complete [this is the twofold goal], thoroughly equipped for every good work" (2 Tim. 3:16-17, NKJV).

The inward goal is mature character, just like that of Jesus. The outward goal is to have the tools one needs to do God's work in this world. That's the purpose of God's Word as it is applied to the life of a growing believer.

Many people shy away from making disciples because they don't think they have enough knowledge of the Bible. Wrong! The last thing your struggling friend needs is for you to be the Bible Answer Man. He or she doesn't need the facts about the Bible you learned in college or in a training program. What he or she does need is to see God's Word lived out in practical application in your life—the Word become flesh.

John tells us that the Word of God "became flesh and dwelt among us, . . . full of grace and truth" (John 1:14, NKJV). That's Jesus he's talking about. He modeled the application of God's truth for us in many different kinds of situations. For example, He didn't just tell us to do the will of God, He showed us His own struggle to put that principle into action. And, in a very real sense, God expects us to do the same: live out God's truth in our everyday lives, allowing the Word of God to become flesh in us. What your friend needs to see and hear is how God's truth made a difference in your life.

When I was 28 I made a very foolish decision: I bought a farm I couldn't manage and didn't need with money I didn't have to impress people I didn't even like. I planned to sell the farm quickly, get rich overnight, and show those people how clever I was. You can guess the outcome. The bottom fell out of the real estate market and I was stuck. I was broke. I couldn't sell the farm without taking a huge loss, and I couldn't pay for it. I was unable to do the other things I wanted because I was tied to this stupid decision. I eventually wound up in the hospital, worn out physically and emotionally. In desperation, I finally turned to Scripture to see if God's Word had anything to say about managing money.

Did it ever! One of the first passages that caught my attention was 1 Tim. 6:9-10: "People who want to get rich fall into temptation and a trap and into many foolish and harmful desires that plunge men into ruin and destruction. For the love of money is a root of all kinds of evil. Some people, eager for money, have wandered from the faith and pierced themselves with many griefs." Yes, I knew all about that. I knew many of those griefs by their common English and Latin names. I was painfully aware of the root of my problem: I tried to get rich quick. So are there other teachings about managing money in the Bible? You bet there are, and I dug them out and began to put them into practice as best I could. I set seven financial goals for myself, based on Scripture, although at the time I didn't see how any of them were possible:

1. Meet my family's needs.
2. Tithe.
3. Pay my taxes on time.

4. Get completely out of debt.

5. Live on a margin (have six months' salary in the bank).

6. Save for future needs and don't spend unless it's already there.

7. Invest the rest for ministry or give it away.

Eight years later, I was astonished to discover that I had met all those goals. In fact, I was asked to write a textbook on Christian financial management. *Moi?* The guy who went broke? Yes, but the secret was in the power of God's truth, not in my own cleverness or brilliance. On my own, I completely messed up.

Now I have one tool in my toolbox to help my friends, at least those friends who are having trouble managing their money or who are tempted to invest in foolish ventures. My experience can be helpful to them because it points them to the proven principles of Scripture, answering not only the "what should I do?" questions but also the "why?" and "how?" Is the effectiveness of my counsel based on something I learned in a class or read in a book? No, it is based on my failure.

I'm pretty good with some other areas too: dealing with bitterness, overcoming depression, and raising three different types of teenagers. Why do you think I can be helpful in those areas? Because I struggled with them and failed in my own strength. But God gave grace and truth in my time of need.

I must confess I'm not very helpful when it comes to

helping people through a divorce. Nor do I have much to offer people who are struggling with the existence of God. Nor am I good at helping friends with alcoholism. Why not? Because I never experienced those problems.

When we lived in Connecticut, I had two friends who had problems with alcoholism: Harold and Bob. I felt I should help them. So, every time Harold would get drunk, he'd call me and we'd talk, somewhat. He'd blubber on and on in his drunken stupor, crying about all the mistakes he'd made in his life. I'd listen patiently, and I'd at least feel good that I was making a sacrificial attempt to help my buddy. Finally, a fellow from Alcoholics Anonymous came to see me. "You're causing Harold more harm than good. You don't know what you're dealing with, so you're simply affirming him in his drinking. Let us deal with Harold." Unfortunately, Harold didn't want to go to AA, and I learned later that he died drunk.

Not long after my encounter with the AA representative, Bob came to see me. Bob was a fine man, a steamfitter, but an alcoholic. He asked for my help. "Bob, I've got just the group for you," I said. "Alcoholics Anonymous."

I moved away from Connecticut, and frankly I forgot about Bob. Twenty-five years later, on a Sunday afternoon, I received a phone call from a lady in Connecticut. "Do you remember a fellow named Bob?" Of course I remembered him, now that my memory was jogged. "Well," she said, "I'm Bob's daughter, and today we're celebrating with my dad 25 years of sobriety. For many of those years he has been the leader of AA for the whole state, and he's helped many, many people overcome their addictions."

I helped Bob. Not by my ingenuity nor even by pointing Bob to passages in the Bible that deal with alcohol. I helped him by acknowledging my inadequacy in that particular area and by pointing him to people who had worked through the problem successfully.

That's the beauty of the network of people we know as the Body of Christ: regardless of the difficulty, somebody in the fellowship has experienced it and dealt with it on the basis of Scripture. The Word of God is incarnate somewhere in my own circle of friends. Wouldn't it be great if I knew the personal stories of all the people I worship with each week? Their testimonies would form a vast repertoire of resources for anyone who might need special assistance in applying God's truth to a particular issue.

So, what's your greatest human asset in making disciples, helping your friends follow Jesus? Your problems! Amazing as it sounds, that's what you have going for you —the fact that you messed up in one area or another. But that's only half true. It's no help to your friend Eddie if you're as unsuccessful in overcoming resentment as he is. You have to first find a solution in Scripture, apply it faithfully to your life, reflect on what God has done to get you through the mess, then call Eddie.

Paul, the first missionary to Europe, had a situation in his life just as troubling as the one that's bothering you right now. He called it "a thorn in my flesh, a messenger of Satan, to torment me" (2 Cor. 12:7). What was this thorn in the flesh? Who knows. It may have been a physical ailment, a great temptation, or a broken relationship. Whatever it was, Paul begged God to take it away, just like you are asking God to remove your current irritation. But God said, "My grace is sufficient for you, for my power is made perfect in weakness" (2 Cor. 12:9). So Paul did a 180-degree turn in his attitude about the thorn in the flesh. He decided to be happy and grateful about it, rather than grumpy and resentful, because it was an opportunity for God to demonstrate His strength.

When you commit yourself to making disciples, it gives you a whole new perspective on your own trials and tribulations. It helps you go through the current difficulty, knowing that on the other side is another tool for your toolbox. After you get through this current puddle, you can guide someone else across.

Listen to Paul, writing about problems he was going through at another time in his life: "Praise be to the God and Father of our Lord Jesus Christ, the Father of compassion and the God of all comfort, who comforts us in all our troubles, so that we can comfort those in any trouble with the comfort we ourselves have received from God" (2 Cor. 1:3-4). He regarded his own troubles as a training ground to help others with the same difficulties. You can do that. You can even give praise and thanks to God that you have experienced heartaches and sufferings, knowing that someone in your circle of friends is going to benefit from your experience. And when you share your insights, your friend will be helped and God will be honored.

The issues that hinder your friends in their walk with Jesus are not the scratches and bruises of life that can be cured by sympathy and bandages. They are deep wounds to the heart and cancerous maladies of the spirit. Even if you are a trained psychologist, you're not capable of addressing those spiritual disorders. You don't have the resources to get to the root of the difficulties. But God's Word is superbly able to reach down into those inner resources of the heart and bring healing and restoration. Again, the writer to the Hebrews assures us, "For the word of God is living and active. Sharper than any double-edged sword, it penetrates even to dividing soul and spirit, joints and marrow; it judges the thoughts and attitudes of the heart" (Heb. 4:12).

Your friend needs help in following Jesus. You can be the instrument God uses to help him or her take even the most difficult step. But the only effective instrument in that process is the powerful sword of God's Word, applied by the Holy Spirit to his or her receptive heart.

## For Reflection and Discussion

1. How does the Word of God "become flesh" in us?

2. According to 2 Tim. 3:17, what is the goal of the application of Scripture to life?

3. In the process of making disciples, why is it helpful to know which kinds of experiences people in the local church have been through?

4. What is the value of learning as many of the promises of God, as revealed in Scripture, that we can learn?

eleven

let

silence

do

the Heavy

lifting

Martha and I often listen to audiobooks when we travel. Before we head out on a long trip, we go to the public library and stock up. Recently, I chose a set of tapes by business consultant Susan Scott. I was intrigued by the title: *Fierce Conversations.* I was so delighted with the fresh insights she presented on conversations that I bought several copies of her book and gave them my friends and colleagues at work.

One chapter in Susan Scott's book is titled "Let Silence Do the Heavy Lifting." As I listened to her description of how silence can be a powerful tool in organizational counseling, it confirmed many of my own thoughts on the value of silence in redemptive friendships. Much of the real progress in the process of making disciples occurs in silence.

Silence has been valued as a personal Christian discipline since the early days of the Church. Meditation and contemplation are high on the list of valuable tools for Christian growth. There is a wealth of literature on the value of silence. My own summertime ritual entails an early morning quiet time. I build a little fire on the rocky shore of our cove, drink my coffee, and think great thoughts—in silence. However, the silence of Christian mysticism is solitary silence, not the poignant silence of intense conversation, which is our subject.

Silence in conversation plays the same role as white space in art, rests in music, and dramatic pauses in oratory. When the mind stops processing words and sounds and

Americans

are

uneasy

with silence

in a

conversation.

images, the heart has room to process meaning. In a good conversation, just as in good music, there is a balance between sound and silence. The pauses bracket the sounds for maximum impact, or is it the other way around?

When I was growing up, I had the privilege of hearing many great preachers: Clovis Chappell, E. Stanley Jones, David Seamands, Paul Rees, John R. Church, and many others. However, none could match the oratory of the great black American preachers. My favorite was E. V. Hill. His sentences were epigrammatic pronouncements—little messages that stood alone—followed by wonderful pauses. His audiences quickly picked up the cadence: statement, pause, statement, pause, statement, pause, building up to a thunderous climax. Then a long pause, as the message had time to settle in. Next he would tell a little story, in a narrative voice, to illustrate the point, then back to the theme from a different perspective. The power was only half in the spoken word; the real impact took place in the empty spaces.

Americans are uneasy with silence in a conversation. Not talking is thought to indicate that you don't have anything to say or that you're not really paying attention or that your mind is somewhere else. We pounce on any slice of silence as an opportunity to say whatever is on our mind, whether or not it is relevant to what has been said before. That's why the flood of conversation we are engaged in every day does not help our friends follow Jesus. We project what we want to say rather than use the entire conversation—words, silence, expressions—to accomplish an important task.

Top-level diplomats earn their positions of leadership by mastering the art of conversations that accomplish something. Any person with a modicum of intelligence can conduct an interesting conversation with a Chinese official. But only the best can guide a conversation to a workable trade agreement, a peace treaty, or a successful negotiation on nuclear proliferation. Conversations that accomplish something take practice and preparation and combine the right setting, timing, mood, nuances, gestures, and especially silence.

When our kids were in grade school we tried to teach them to be good conversationalists by playing "conversational catch." We'd stand in the yard and throw a softball back and forth. The first person would make a statement, then toss the ball to the other. That child then had to repeat the first person's statement in a different form, then add a new statement that built on the first, then toss the ball back to the first and so on.

One evening, a fellow from out of town dropped by for a visit. He was full of himself. He never stopped talking, from the time he stepped through the door until we ushered him out. He waxed on and on about his accomplishments, all the places he'd traveled, his hobbies, his family, and so on. When the door was finally closed behind him, our son Joe said, "Whew! That guy was playing conversational burnout!"

The last thing our growing Christian friends need is conversational burnout. They don't need to hear you or me display our vast repertoire of learning or experience. They do need a conversational environment where faith and obedience can grow. That environment entails silence.

Jesus chose ideal environments to help His friends step outside their religious and cultural comfort zones. He took them into cross-cultural situations and into arenas where there was a clear distinction between the kingdom of God and the ways of this world. He led them through towns and villages crowded with needy people, into life-threatening situations that demanded faith, and into remote regions where they were totally alone. In every situation, He made sure there were quiet times when His disciples had opportunity to assimilate what He was teaching.

Susan Scott says in her book, "The more emotion there is attached to an issue, the more we need to rely on silence."* Silence allows our friend to hear the still small voice of God's Spirit in the spaces between the words. The longer the silences, the more he or she will hear God's voice instead of ours.

An incident popped into my mind about the value of silence: One day I was walking from my office at the university to the parking lot. At the edge of the lot I noticed a young woman, presumably a student, sitting on the

---

*Susan Scott, *Fierce Conversations* (New York: Berkley Books, 2002), 224.

ground, curled up with her head between her knees. I knew right away this girl was having serious problems, so I asked, "Are you OK?" No response. I asked again. Nothing. I lifted up her head and saw that her eyes were glazed over in a vacant stare. The lights were on, but nobody home. I started back to my office to call the college clinic, but as an afterthought I took the girl's hand and wrote on her palm with my ballpoint pen: "Come see me" and also wrote my office number.

I did call the clinic, and again the next morning phoned to see how she was doing. "Her name is Becky, and we've been treating her for several weeks. The doctors and psychologists have checked her over, and she's experiencing severe depression. We're going to have to send her home because she's not getting better. It's really a shame, because she's been a straight A student until now, but she's so heavily medicated she can't even stay awake in class. She's a zombie."

That afternoon I looked through the open door of my office, and there stood Becky. I had looked up her photo in the college yearbook.

"Come in," I said. But she just stood there, like she was unable to move.

"Come in and have a seat." And I led her to a chair and sat her down. I returned to my desk, whispered a quick prayer for wisdom, then asked, "What's the problem?"

She just sat there, looking blankly at the floor. I knew I could offer her no professional help; she'd already been treated by very capable medical and psychiatric people. So I decided to let silence work. I just sat there, not even glancing at the pile of papers on my desk waiting to be graded. There was no sound for 45 minutes. Forty-five minutes! You know, 5 minutes of silence is almost beyond endurance for most Americans, but 45! However, I resisted the temptation to talk.

Finally, she said in a barely audible voice, "I can't cope."

"Can't cope with what?" I asked. And we sat for another long period of silence, perhaps half an hour.

Finally, she began to whisper, then to talk very hesitatingly. I just listened. She had a younger sister on whom her parents doted. Apparently her sister was Miss Everything—beautiful, talented, and popular. Becky was the ugly duckling, at least in her own mind, and her parents had shown favoritism. However, Becky had one advantage: she was a brilliant student. She had been valedictorian of her high school class and came to college on a full academic scholarship.

"But I got mononucleosis at the beginning of this semester and couldn't keep up. By the time I got well enough to attend class, I was too far behind. I knew I was going to flunk out, and I got more and more depressed. It was a total downward spiral, with no way out."

We opened God's Word together and worked through several passages of Scripture that indeed do offer ways out of every dilemma in which we find ourselves. I called her professors and asked if Becky could take incompletes in her courses, with the assurance she could make up the work later. They agreed. I also asked if she had any Christian friends, classmates who could give her encouragement and support. "I used to attend a Presbyterian church, but I haven't been to worship since I came to college. And I've been so absorbed in my studies, I haven't made many friends." I arranged for a fellow who attended a nearby Presbyterian church to make sure she got to Sunday services and was included in their social activities.

A few weeks later I noticed that this fellow was giving her much more attention than I had requested. He was going far beyond the call of duty, ushering her around campus and carrying her books. And she was glowing. She was blossoming into a real beauty, accepting who she was in Christ and who she was in the eyes of an adoring friend. Years later, I learned that they were married, serving the Lord together as public schoolteachers, and leading members of a good Presbyterian Church.

Silence plays a great part in critical conversations. White spaces are important in every conversation, but they are essential for progress in matters of the heart. In the context of an ongoing friendship between growing Christians, silence can be a powerful tool. In the music of relationships, the rests are as important as the notes, the silences as important as the words.

## For Reflection and Discussion

1. What is the value of silence in conversation?

2. Why do most people avoid blank spaces in everyday talk?

3. How did Jesus use silence as a teaching tool?

4. What happens during the silences in conversation?

twelve

man

to Man,

woman to

woman

A man needs a friend—one who sticks closer than a brother. He needs a wider circle of like-minded men with whom he shares deep loyalties and common goals. And he needs an even broader network of buddies—fellow travelers on the road to Christian maturity. This is his base; he can't develop fully without them. These are his fellow pilgrims who will encourage his growth and keep him steady.

Sure, there is a healthy balance between activities that are "for men only" and those that are mixed. However, the crying need of today's church is for an environment where men can establish deep friendships with other men. There are aspects of a man's development that can only take place in that brotherly arena where "iron sharpens iron" (Prov. 27:17).

Men need to work on projects together: fix cars, go to ball games, hunt, climb mountains, study. Their comradeship on these ventures forms a basis on which Christian discipleship can develop. Just as Paul took young men along with him on his missionary journeys, so men today are motivated by serving together on important endeavors. There's nothing like the sound of 25,000 men singing "Amazing Grace" at the top of their lungs at a Promise-Keepers rally to give a man the inspiration he needs to go home and be a good husband, father, and church member.

I've climbed Mount Kilimanjaro in Tanzania three times in the company of bands of men and their half-grown sons. There was a camaraderie established on those thin-air safaris that left a deep imprint on my spirit and hopefully on the lives of my climbing companions. A team of men, bound together in a common mission, have a profound impact on each other. When that mission is a Christian one, and the brothers are committed to following Jesus, that can be a powerful motivational influence.

Not that there aren't competent women who can climb mountains, fix cars, and hunt elk; it's just that there's a special environment created when all the participants are men. The same is equally true when the activities and relationships are exclusively for women, although I'm certainly not qualified to address the special needs of women in interaction with other women.

I'm often asked, "Should women teach men?" My answer is: "Yes, certainly; and absolutely not!" I'm not dithering, I'm just answering two different questions. The pivotal word is *teach*. If the question is, "Should women have a teaching role in the church when men are part of the audience?" The answer is "of course!" Many of the church's finest Bible teachers, theologians, and public speakers are women. On the local church level, the percentage is even higher.

However, when it comes to making disciples, person-to-person, one conversation at a time, I am adamant: man-to-man, woman-to-woman. I'll list several reasons why this must be the rule:

1. The process of making a disciple, helping a friend follow Jesus, requires a deep personal relationship.

The art of bringing the Word of God to bear on the "thoughts and intents of the heart" (Heb. 4:12, NKJV) requires a level of intimacy that is not appropriate for a man to share with any woman other than his wife. The barriers to healthy discipleship are bedrock habits and thought patterns that lie far beneath the surface. They cannot be addressed through a casual relationship.

When I was in seminary, pastoral counseling was quite the rage. We were all taught how to delve into the deep, dark secrets of the lives of our troubled parishioners, women as well as men. Some good may have come from all that, but the overall effect on church leadership has been devastating. Thousands of pastors have been washed out of the ministry, including some of the finest and most prominent, because they became entangled in a web of intimacy with women counselees. And some fine women leaders have succumbed to the same trap.

A couple years ago I attended a pastors' conference at one of our leading seminaries. One seminar leader was conducting a discussion titled "The Pastor's Personal Spiritual Life." He asked his class, "If a pastor is counseling a woman who is having trouble in her marriage, and he begins to feel an emotional attraction toward her, how does he maintain his personal commitment to a holy life?" After several inane suggestions had been made, I couldn't keep quiet. I stood up and shocked the audience by saying, "I can't think of any reason why a male pastor should be counseling a woman, and I can give you a dozen reasons why he shouldn't."

The seminar leader was aghast. "Just give one reason why a pastor shouldn't offer counseling to a woman who sincerely requests help."

"I'll give you two," I said. "Wayne and Ed. They attended this same conference with us last year; now they've both crashed. Both of them were fine pastors and members of our fellowship. Now their ministries are ruined, their families are wrecked, and they've become another reason why unbelievers don't trust the church. They got involved with women they were counseling. Any pastor who claims he can counsel an attractive woman who is emotionally needy is either more than a man or less than a man."

The leader quickly switched to another topic, but several attendees accosted me in the hall afterward. One so-called pastor said, "If I didn't counsel women, how would I spend my time? That's what I do every day." Good grief!

I am following Jesus today, thanks to the investment made in my life by godly men who loved me enough to pierce my surface defenses. They cultivated such a heart-to-heart relationship with me that I could be secure enough to reveal my innermost spiritual struggles. When they got to that level of friendship with me, I was able to make some genuine progress. The deep personal fellowship I enjoyed with those men was not only appropriate but also essential for me to grow spiritually. It would not have been appropriate to have that kind of relationship with any woman, regardless of her spiritual maturity.

2. A man who disciples or counsels women robs Christian women of their biblical role in ministry. The apostle Paul highlighted the function of godly women in his letter to Titus, chapter 2. In a healthy, disciple-building church, women should shoulder a major portion of the ministry. At least half the primary ministry of the church is theirs: bringing other women to maturity in Christ.

    Many of our churches today are weak and ineffective because there is not a well-trained, fully equipped corps of women who are effective in making disciples. We have fine schools and effective training for pastors, church administrators, musicians, and youth workers. But who is training women to equip other women in the church's No. 1 priority: making disciples?

3. Helping a friend follow Jesus entails applying spiritual pressure. We'll deal with this in another chap-

ter, but at this point suffice it to say that it isn't appropriate for a woman to hold a man's feet to the fire or for a man to confront a woman on her failure to live up to her commitments. I fully expect that my godly male friends (or my own wife) will call me to account for my behavior, but it is not healthy for those same men to put pressure on my wife or vice versa.

There are a handful of men whom I will travel halfway across the country to spend personal time with. I know they will tell me the truth, whether I like it or not, and I value that relationship. Last year, I met up with David Kilel, chaplain at Tenwek Hospital in Kenya and a longtime friend. The first question he asked me, in front of my whole team, was, "What have you learned from the mistakes you made in the _____ project?" He has earned the right to tighten the screws on me, to make sure I'm learning from my mistakes. It is part of our mutual disciple-building relationship for him to confront me about deeply personal failures. It is not appropriate for him to put that kind of pressure on my wife, nor for me to challenge Esta's (his wife's) behavior.

4. Counseling a woman will drive her husband away from the church. Suppose you're a nonbelieving fellow whose wife has recently started attending church. She comes home and announces, "I've

shared with my pastor all the problems we've been having in our marriage. I want you to come to church with me." No way is that guy going to come listen to that pastor preach.

However, if mature women in the fellowship have taken that new Christian wife under their wings and taught her "what is good" as directed in Titus 2:3-5, that skeptical husband will be far more open to the gospel.

5. A man having a one-to-one conversation alone with a woman (other than his wife) sends the wrong signal. It raises too many questions, even if it is entirely legitimate. Most of the top-level Christian leaders I know will not allow themselves to be in any situation alone with a woman, especially in a closed-door setting.

One of the best atmospheres for making disciples in our culture is to meet someone for lunch or breakfast. I do this several times a week. And I'm gratified to see other men from my church meeting other men in the same restaurant, or women praying with other women. That's what is supposed to happen when the church is penetrating the community with the transforming truth of the gospel. But it causes me concern when I see a woman, whatever the reason, meeting alone with a man who isn't her husband.

6. A woman cannot be the model for Christian man-

hood. Nor can a man demonstrate to a woman all she should become in Christ. Modeling is the finest kind of training. That's why the standards for leadership in the church are so high (1 Tim. 3, Titus 2): when a leader stands before the church, who that person is carries more significance than what he or she says.

7. I often say jokingly, "A man who claims he understands women will lie about everything else." While that may be said in jest, there is a great deal of truth in the fact that men and women communicate differently. I am no expert in male/female learning styles, but I am observant enough to know that spoken words are interpreted in gender-specific ways.

I have four wonderful women in my life, only one of which I had any part in choosing myself: my wife, Martha. The other three just happened: my two daughters and my delightful daughter-in-law. I listen in wonder as they communicate with each other and with the various women in whose lives they are investing. Honestly, I try my best to communicate with them, but frequently I'm reminded that I just don't get it. We use the same set of common English words, but the nuances aren't the same.

Remember, the goal of making disciples is not just getting facts from my notebook into theirs, it is the process of establishing lifelong friendships for the furtherance of God's kingdom. The deep bonding that takes place between intimate friends is too important to jeopardize with unnecessary temptations.

Friendships are the bedrock on which sturdy character is built. The woman is rich who has one or two or three intimate women friends who share her convictions and encourage her growth. A boy is most blessed who has a buddy his age or a Scout leader or a father or a man in his church who will walk with him through the tough growing-up years. A girl needs a female friend to whom she can unburden her soul. And a man whose friends are willing to lay down their lives for his spiritual development has this world's most coveted treasure.

## For Reflection and Discussion

1. Should women teach men in the church?

2. What are some of the dangers of men "discipling" women?

3. What can the church do to help men develop healthy friendships?

thirteen

the

"one anothers"

of making

# Disciples

Some of the functions required in the process of making disciples occur in church—"church" meaning the gathered assembly of people for worship. A person who has made a sincere commitment to follow Jesus can receive both information and inspiration to continue his or her growth as a disciple by attending church services. However, many of the essential ingredients for spiritual development cannot be found in any large gathering. They require a completely different setting.

Those tools for making disciples are called "the one anothers" because they appear in the New Testament with that description. *One* is the focus—one person at a time. And each of these tools is used one specific application at a time—usually in one conversation. The *other* is a friend for whom a caring Christian takes personal spiritual responsibility.

Most churches do not grow spiritually or numerically for two reasons: very few church members take the initiative to assume responsibility for their friends' spiritual growth. They have never heard that making disciples is their duty and privilege, even though this was a central teaching of Jesus. Second, the "one anothers" require small intimate associations to work—either small groups that stay together for an extended period of time or one-to-one relationships. Not many churches know how to foster these productive little groupings, which is one reason for this book.

The "one anothers" are the curriculum of spiritual

growth. *Curriculum* is a Latin word that means "race-track." A racetrack has some basic elements: a starting point, a finish line, boundaries, and rules. Educational experts describe a curriculum in terms of its scope and sequence, that is, the range of material or skills to be mastered and the order. In most cases, a curriculum is a set of ordered steps toward a predetermined goal.

Did Jesus have a curriculum in mind when He trained those first 12 disciples? You bet He did! The knowledge content of His teaching was the principles of the kingdom of God. The relational content was how to follow Him and get along with each other. The starting point was their decision to accept His invitation to follow Him, and the goal was the personal transformation of their lives and the establishment of His kingdom on earth.

Jesus chose two different instructional settings for His training in Kingdom living: formal and nonformal. The formal arena was public presentations to large groups of people, like the Sermon on the Mount. The nonformal environment was personal interaction with the small group of 12 as they walked along. The experiences of everyday life were used as object lessons to illustrate the principles of the Kingdom and to drill them into the working habits of His followers. And, from time to time, He took one or another of His friends apart and conducted intensive personal discussions.

The apostle Paul and the leaders of the Early Church at Jerusalem followed this same pattern: public worship, pri-

love

is an

Affectionate

commitment

built on

mutual respect.

vate discipling. When Paul went to the city of Thessalonica, he did three things every day: he proclaimed the gospel publicly, he worked for a living making tents, and he gave intense personal care to individuals. He describes his relationship with them as a mother caring for her babies or a father encouraging his children. And his goal was clear: "urging you to live lives worthy of God, who calls you into his kingdom and glory" (1 Thess. 2:12; read vv. 1-12).

You, too, have everything you need to make disciples: clear instructions in Scripture, the assignment given to you by Jesus himself, and friends who are ready and willing to grow. The amazing fact about this curriculum is that it is universal: it works whether you're living in Manhattan or the jungles of Borneo. It works among university graduates and people who are completely illiterate. It worked in the first century, it works now, and it will work in 2525. You probably go to work every day to earn a living, just like the apostle Paul did. You can extend Jesus' domain over the hearts and lives of your friends, just like Jesus, Paul, and the apostles did. Just find a friend, and follow the "one another" directions in Scripture.

All the "one another" tools cluster around the central command Jesus gave His disciples: love one another. Love is an affectionate commitment built on mutual respect. Jesus did not merely suggest that we love each other, He commanded it over and over. Loving other believers is not an option, it is an absolute requirement. And if we love our friend, we will express that affection by practicing the "one another" disciplines with him or her. When we do that, Jesus said the world will know that we are His disciples.

A first-time visitor to a local church on a typical Sunday morning will not likely see this kind of love expressed. Not because the Christians in that particular church don't love each other but because big gatherings are not the showcase for Christian love. The world will know that we are Christians when they see it expressed in personal friendships. When they see us laying down our lives for each other, they are much more likely to believe in a Savior who laid down His life for His friends. They will see this as two sisters meet in a coffee shop to bear one another's burdens or instruct one another or encourage one another. They will see God's love in action when one businessman meets another in his office to spur him on to love and good deeds.

There are more than 40 "one another" tools in Scripture, all of them radiating from the central hub of loving one another. I group them in four categories: preconditional, instructional, relational, and housekeeping "one anothers." By "preconditional" I mean those elements of a friend-to-friend relationship that are determined before the relationship ever begins. They are the foundation on which strong relationships are built.

The first preconditional "one another" is honor, also known as respect, esteem, and valuing another person as important, even before introductions are made. One specific reference is Rom. 12:10, but the principle is found throughout Scripture. In fact the first commandment with a promise is "Honor your father and your mother" (Exod. 20:12). A child learning to honor his or her parents is learning the skill essential to every other relationship in life: marriage, student/teacher, employee/employer, friend/friend. All great friendships are built on honor.

I'm often asked, "What's the most important skill a person needs in order to work in another culture?" People are usually astonished at my answer: "Honor. And you learn it by honoring your father and mother. An African can read it in your eyes. He can tell from across the room whether or not you honor him. If you have it, you will have a good start for successful cross-cultural relationships. If you don't, a Ph.D. in anthropology won't enable you to really connect and make friends with someone from a different culture." *Honor* means genuine respect, and it has to be developed before the other "one anothers" can have an effect.

The next one is "Greet one another with a holy kiss" (Rom. 16:16). In our culture we don't do much kissing when we greet, but the principle is still valid: how you greet someone conditions the future relationship. A cold, stiff greeting may be correct, but it is insufficient. An over-zealous, pushy, loud, or gushy greeting can be just as negative. Greet people with your eyes first, then a firm handshake that says, "I look forward to knowing you better, if that is appropriate."

Here's a hard one: the willingness to be inconvenienced. Paul admonished the Christians at Corinth: "So then, my brothers, when you come together to eat, wait for each other" (1 Cor. 11:33). I know he was specifically referring to the logistics of the Communion fellowship, but the principle of *willingness to wait* is an important one. Businessmen with whom I've made an appointment for lunch often stand me up or fail to arrive on time. I put up with the inconvenience for two reasons: (1) the opportunity to establish a disciple-building relationship is worth the risk of wasting my time, and (2) I remember those men who waited for me to show up in the early days of my own spiritual pilgrimage. Where would I be today if they hadn't been willing to wait?

Also, Paul had to remind his friends to "not be proud, but be willing to associate with people of low position" (Rom. 12:16). James, the leader of the Church at Jerusalem, has a whole section of his letter dedicated to this subject (James 2). This is not a decision we make on the spot; it is a frame of mind that is established far in advance and affects every new person we meet.

The next set of "one anothers" is a toolbox full of relational equipment. There's a long list of specific guidelines for getting along with each other, including extensive sections of New Testament books that address those specific issues. For example: "Be kind and compassionate to one another, forgiving each other, just as Christ in God forgave you" (Eph. 4:32). "Make sure that nobody pays back wrong for wrong" (1 Thess. 5:15). "Do not slander one another" (James 4:11). "Clothe yourselves with humility toward one another" (1 Pet. 5:5).

One of the most important of these relational principles, given first by Jesus then repeated several times in the New Testament, is not to judge. That is, we are not to condemn others for their behavior. The penalty for disobeying this command is stiff: we will be judged exactly as we judge others.

The word *judge* comes from the Greek word that means "to observe, evaluate, or assess." It is the same root from which we get the word *discern,* which we are always to do. So what's the difference between discerning and judging? If one comes with great reward and the other with dire warnings, we'd better be able to tell them apart.

They both start with a realistic assessment of a situation in someone's life. It's good to make assessments, especially of our own behavior. However, at that point we must make a decision: will we judge or condemn? If we are discerning, we ask, "Is there an appropriate way for me to help in this situation?" If not, leave it alone. If we judge, we condemn the other person by attacking, talking about, or writing off that person and isolating ourselves from him or her. Don't do that; it will come back to haunt you and it will kill the opportunity for making a disciple.

One more: "Make up your mind not to put any stumbling block or obstacle in your brother's way" (Rom. 14:13). This means that sometimes we have to limit our freedom to accommodate our friend's sensitivity on some issue. Often it is some cultural practice about which there is no specific scriptural prohibition. In Paul's day the big squabble was over eating meat that had been offered to idols. Paul spelled out an elaborate argument about why there was no problem eating this meat, but then he says he won't do it so as not to offend the "weaker brother" (see 1 Cor. 8:9 and Gal. 5:13). Use good judgment and diplomacy.

Then there are some instructional "one anothers," tools for helping our friends grow in their spiritual lives. They are fairly self-evident, so I'll just list them with a brief comment:

1. "Instruct one another" (Rom. 15:14).
2. "Agree with one another so that there may be no divisions among you" (1 Cor. 1:10).
3. "Bear one another's burdens" (Eph. 4:2, NKJV).
4. "Speak to one another with psalms, hymns and spiritual songs" (Eph. 5:19).
5. "Admonish one another with all wisdom" (Col. 3:16).
6. "Encourage one another" (1 Thess. 5:11 and Heb. 3:13).
7. "Spur one another on toward love and good deeds" (Heb. 10:24).
8. "Confess your sins to one another, and pray for each other" (James 5:16, NASB).

Finally, some of the "one anothers" are what I would call housekeeping chores—tasks that need to be done to keep the fellowship working happily. One of the mistakes that often kills a disciple-building relationship is loaning money. Don't do it. If a friend needs food or shelter, give it to him, but don't lend him a dime. Paul said to his friends, "Let no debt remain outstanding, except the continuing debt to love one another" (Rom. 13:8).

"Let us not give up meeting together" the writer of Hebrews warns (10:25). Just because you're in a specialized ministry or enjoying a terrific one-to-one relationship, don't quit going to church.

The housekeeping ministry I most appreciate is "Offer hospitality to one another without grumbling" (1 Pet. 4:9). Hospitality was considered a primary qualification for leadership in the Early Church (1 Tim. 3:2 and Titus 1:8). Gaius, to whom the letter of 3 John is addressed, was singled out for praise by John because of the kind hospitality he had shown to traveling Christians.

The thread that runs through all the "one another" admonitions is love. Love is the driving force behind redemptive relationships. It turns casual friendships into opportunities to expand God's kingdom one conversation at a time. And "love covers over a multitude of sins" (1 Pet. 4:8). Whatever else that may mean, it reassures those of us who are trying to help our friends follow Jesus that our mistakes will be overlooked if we love our friends enough.

## For Reflection and Discussion

1. Name as many of the "one anothers" of Scripture as you can.

2. What context is required for the "one anothers" to be applied?

3. What is the basic, central "one another"—the one on which all the others are founded?

4. What three things did the apostle Paul do every day (as recorded in 2 Thess. 2)?

5. How is a curriculum like a racetrack?

fourteen

# Visualizing

## the

# next
# steps

Here's an idea that is as timeless as the letters of the New Testament, yet as timely as today's sports page: visualize spiritual progress as though it has already been achieved. If you and your friend are sincere in your quest to follow Jesus, this tool can enhance your conversations. First, I'll tell you what the sports trainers have discovered, then we'll see how Jesus and His followers used the same technique.

Sports psychology is a new science built around the discovery of an old reality: human beings can improve their performance of any task by first envisioning it perfectly in their minds. If a figure skater has a complicated Olympic routine to perform, a coach helps that person visualize a perfect presentation. Once that image has been firmly established, the coach and the skater play the mental video over and over. The coach talks the athlete through every move. The skater hears the music in perfect synchronization with each movement and feels the exhilaration of a spin, an axel, a toe loop perfectly executed. The skater hears the crowd cheering, sees them standing to their feet, and hears his or her name called to come to the dais. The skater hears his or her national anthem playing, sees the coach smiling, and feels the sash with the gold medal being hung around his or her neck. Over and over the skater mentally rehearses this video. When that person actually goes onto the ice, he or she performs the routine exactly as it was imagined so many times before.

Jesus did this with His disciples. At the outset of their relationship He established a vision of a future in which their lives would be entirely different: "Follow me, . . . and I will make you fishers of men" (Matt. 4:19). Those fellows probably never dreamed of influencing other people, never saw themselves as anything but fishermen. But Jesus painted a picture of them as fishers of men long before they became anything like that. He envisioned spiritual achievement for them. Once the picture was etched into their minds, they could become what He wanted (and they wanted) them to be.

Paul did the same with his friends. We don't have transcripts of their conversations, but we do have letters, and those letters reveal a powerful character-shaping tool. He visualized spiritual progress for them. He painted a word picture of what they could become and framed that picture in prayer. Listen to his prayer for his friends in Ephesus:

> I keep asking that the God of our Lord Jesus Christ, the glorious Father, may give you the Spirit of wisdom and revelation, so that you may know him better. I pray also that the eyes of your heart may be enlightened in order that you may know the hope to which he has called you, the riches of his glorious inheritance in the saints, and his incomparably great power for us who believe *(Eph. 1:17-19)*.

> I pray that out of his glorious riches he may strengthen you with power through his Spirit in your inner being, so that Christ may dwell in your hearts through faith. And I pray that you, being rooted and es-

tablished in love, may have power, together with all the saints, to grasp how wide and long and high and deep is the love of Christ, and to know this love that surpasses knowledge—that you may be filled to the measure of all the fullness of God. Now to him who is able to do immeasurably more than all we ask or imagine, according to his power that is at work within us, to him be glory in the church and in Christ Jesus throughout all generations, for ever and ever! Amen *(3:16-21)*.

In chapter 4 of that same letter, Paul imagines a wonderful fellowship existing in Ephesus in which all the believers:

- spoke truthfully to each other
- handled anger correctly
- worked productively with their hands
- avoided all unwholesome talk, and
- lived happily together in kindness, compassion, and forgiveness

Were they there yet? No, but they could begin to be if they saw the potential clearly. Once the picture of spiritual maturity was planted in their minds, the actualization of it was far more possible. The men and women addressed in those letters were ordinary people who accomplished extraordinary things because someone, the apostle Paul in this case, drew a picture of spiritual maturity and effective ministry in their minds.

Most of us need help seeing over the sides of our personal rut. We can't imagine being or doing anything much different than we are doing today. That's the function of a redemptive friend—to help visualize progress.

The writer to the Hebrews instructed the early Christians to "encourage one another daily, as long as it is called Today, so that none of you may be hardened by sin's deceitfulness" (Heb. 3:13). The sin that most frequently keeps us from being and doing God's will is unbelief—failure to trust God's plan for our lives. The antidote to that poison is encouragement, and encouragement has to be administered by someone else. We can't do it ourselves.

Your Christian friend needs your encouragement to trust God, to see His plan, and to do it. How often? Every day! Why can't he or she do it alone? Because self-defense mechanisms are so strong we rationalize away bad thinking and poor behavior. And because God created us to need each other.

So how do we encourage our friends? By offering consolation when they grieve and hurt. By celebrating every spiritual victory and achievement. By cheering them on in the race. By standing with them when the going gets tough. By keeping the ideal of God's best before them. By visualizing spiritual progress.

For the past 40 years I've studied Christian workers: spiritual leaders, influential teachers, effective missionaries. When I get the opportunity, I often ask, "What was the spark that ignited your passion? Who inspired you to get started on your mission?" The most common story is this: at some critical time in their lives, usually between the ages of 10 and 20, someone saw potential in them they couldn't see themselves. Occasionally it was a parent who gave them the impetus to strive for a high goal, but usually it was an older Christian friend who provided a picture of a fruitful future.

One of my heroes was Dawson Trotman, founder of the Navigators. His biography, *Daws,* is chock-full of stories of how he influenced young men to spiritual effectiveness. Some of his early successes, men who went on to accomplish great things for God's kingdom, were boys he gathered into a Bible study at the station where he was pumping gas.

In the 1970s I was working with some educational innovators in Guatemala. One night as we sat by lamplight I asked one of the key leaders, "What was the spark that got you started?" He started into a story, variations of which I had heard many times: "I was in the Navy, attending Bible study aboard ship led by Navigators. One day . . ." I stopped him: "Let me finish the story. I think I already know what happened next."

"How can you finish it, when you've never heard it?" he asked.

"I've heard it many times," I said. "One day you met Dawson Trotman and you got a new vision of what you could accomplish if you were totally surrendered to Christ."

"That's exactly what happened," he admitted. "You know, I spent only half an hour with that man, but it changed my life."

What did Dawson Trotman do? He helped his friends see what they could become—in Christ. What did he do that you can't do? Nothing. You are surrounded by people just waiting for someone to come along who can lift their sights above their current situation.

You may not be able to spend hours with the teenagers you meet in church every week, but you can give them a blessing. "John, you're God's ambassador over there at Central High School. I just pray He will help you to let your light shine." "Melissa, you're such a great nursery worker! May the Lord bless your efforts for the Kingdom."

Sometimes it's hard to visualize positive outcomes for people in their present condition, but ability grows with practice. Eventually, we can help people imagine a bright future, even out of negative situations.

Some time back a teenage girl went to a party, got drunk, and came home pregnant. She was ashamed to go back to church. "All the people I considered my friends told me what I already knew: that I had messed up badly. Some were at least nice enough to say they would pray for me, but they avoided me like the plague. Then one day a lady in our church, whom I barely knew, came up to me, put one arm around me and the other on my tummy. She blessed my baby and prayed that the new life within me would bring glory to God and great good to people. She prayed that I would be a great mom and a model to other girls who were going through the same problem. That gave me a vision of what I could do. You ask me how I got the vision for my ministry: a kind lady gave it to me."

Last year I visited an orphanage in northern Malawi. There were 87 kids in this particular center, but one caught my eye. Her name was Grace, and she exuded graciousness. She had an angelic face, bright eyes, and a zest for life. I asked the houseparents: "Tell me about Grace."

"She and her sister were brought in here by villagers who found them living in the street. Their parents apparently died of AIDS, and these girls were emaciated, riddled with parasites, and had never been to school, even though Grace was 10 years old and her sister 12. Grace failed her first term in school because she was so far behind, but she was determined to do better. During the next term, she just blossomed, earned first place in her class, and she's been first ever since."

I went with the houseparents around to tuck all the kids in for the night, pray with them, and give them a goodnight hug. We came to the little room Grace shared with five other girls. I asked Grace the same question I asked the other kids, "What will you be when you grow up and leave the children's home?"

Grace didn't hesitate one second: "A lawyer."

"Tell me, Grace, what you will look like when you are a lawyer?"

"I will stand before the judge and say, 'These poor people have been mistreated. They have no one to speak for them. I will speak for them so they can get what is fair and right.' And they will be happy about that."

Grace could see it. She could hear it, taste it, smell it. I sincerely believe Grace will become what she envisions in her mind. At least she will become more than a waif wandering the streets, eating out of garbage cans. And I credit those godly Malawian houseparents who encouraged her to nurture a noble vision in her heart.

Henrietta Mears was an influential Christian educator who instilled vision in the minds of the youth in her church. One of those young men was Bill Bright, the founder of Campus Crusades, whose ministry has affected millions of people around the world. He kept a photo of Miss Mears on his desk throughout his ministry. Why? Because she was a great teacher? No, because she instilled in him a great vision. She helped him see what nobody else could see: that he could reach an entire world with the gospel.

One of the best definitions of the word *faith* is "visualizing what God intends and cooperating with Him to accomplish that vision." Faith doesn't begin with me, it begins with God. The foundation of our faith is not something we have within ourselves—something that, if we have enough of it, will enable us to get what we want. No, faith is our response to the plan of God, which we discover in His Word. We step out on His promises in order to accomplish His will, not our own. Once we see it, He gives His strength (grace) to make it reality. We are saved by grace, through faith. We do His work in the world by grace, through faith, and in the process we are transformed into His image by grace, through faith.

Christians have long believed that the finest gift we can give our friends is an understanding of the purpose of God for their lives and how to be a part of that plan by faith. However, for many the understanding of that gift is too limited. They see God's gift only in terms of a transaction—the granting of eternal life. God's gift is a total transformation. When the apostle Paul wrote to his friends at Ephesus, he spent the entire first half (three chapters) of his letter outlining the eternal plan of God. The second half is a visualization of the practical steps entailed in making that transformation a daily reality.

## For Reflection and Discussion

1. How did the apostle Paul visualize spiritual progress for his friends?

2. Why is the vision of a young person's potential a key ingredient in the development of Christian leadership?

3. What danger is there in visualizing the future for our own children?

4. What is the relationship between "faith" and "vision"?

# fifteen

# leading

## from a

# Position

## of weakness

I was struggling with a personal problem, so I called my friend John and asked for his help. I described my dilemma, then waited for his response. "This is a problem Christians shouldn't have," he said quickly. "When I was tempted, I just prayed and the Lord delivered me, according to His Word."

I said in frustration, "John, you're always so victorious; you're absolutely no help at all to me. I need to hear how somebody has struggled through this kind of trouble, tried various solutions that didn't work, then finally found the answer."

Redemptive conversations demand an entirely different kind of leadership. We must learn to lead from a position of weakness, not one of superior knowledge or perfect performance. People with real-life problems are not interested in what we read in a book or learned in Bible college. They want to know how we dealt with the same or similar problem in our own lives and found real, personal answers.

This puts a radically different angle on the problems and difficulties we face every day. If we are totally focused on ourselves, problems are obstacles to overcome, irritations to endure, or bad experiences to put behind us. There is no positive value to them. However, if we are investing in others, making disciples, personal trials and painful hurts are our greatest resource.

What? How can problems be our greatest resource?

The apostle Paul said the same thing. In his opening

statement to the struggling Christians at Corinth (2 Cor. 1:3-6), he explains the value of suffering:

> Praise be to the God and Father of our Lord Jesus Christ, the Father of compassion and the God of all comfort, who comforts us in all our troubles, so that we can comfort those in any trouble with the comfort we ourselves have received from God. For just as the sufferings of Christ flow over into our lives, so also through Christ our comfort overflows. If we are distressed, it is for your comfort and salvation; if we are comforted, it is for your comfort, which produces in you patient endurance of the same sufferings we suffer.

That doesn't mean those terrible experiences are good in themselves, but they do provide a basis for serving others in need. In his troubles, Paul was enabled to overcome by the "God of all comfort," so that he in turn could comfort his friends.

The clearest example from Paul's life is what he called "a thorn in my flesh" (2 Cor. 12:7; see vv. 7-10). We don't know exactly what this "thorn" was (some have speculated it was a physical ailment), but we can all identify with Paul. We all have thorns—a rebellious child, a serious disability, a deep hurt, a financial disaster. Initially, Paul handled his thorn as we all tend to do—he resented it and asked God to remove it.

However, God used Paul's thorn to teach him a powerful lesson about grace. Grace is the power of God's love, available to His children to handle any problem. It is not only the means of our eternal salvation but also the moment-by-moment strength that enables us to follow Jesus every day, every step of the way. The Word of the Lord, to Paul and to us, is, "My grace is sufficient for you, for my power is made perfect in weakness" (v. 9).

Grace cast Paul's thorn in the flesh in a different light. Not only was his thorn not a liability to his ministry; but it was an asset as well. So, Paul did a turnabout in his attitude toward the "thorn in my flesh." He came to see that his "weaknesses, . . . insults, . . . hardships, . . . persecutions, [and] . . . difficulties" (v. 10) were assets in the business of making disciples, not liabilities. He decided to delight in them, even brag about them. Why? Because everywhere he was weak, Christ could be strong; everywhere he was defeated, Christ could prove himself the Victor.

That's the nature of grace. Grace can only work when we acknowledge that we can't solve a problem by our own cleverness, resourcefulness, creativity, or strength. Our Heavenly Father makes His grace available only when we admit we can't do it ourselves, for "God opposes the proud but gives grace to the humble" (1 Pet. 5:5).

Now let's talk about your problem and how it relates to the business of making disciples. When it comes to helping your friends follow Jesus, your greatest resource is your record of failure and defeat. Incredible as it may sound, the unique set of problems you have faced in your lifetime is a gold mine. They are the foundation on which your ministry to your friends should be built. Every thorn in the flesh you have experienced should be (first) an opportunity for God to show himself strong in your weakness and (second) a resource with which to help others who face a similar failure.

Let me give an example: we have a wonderful lady in our church named Michelle (Shelly) Weiss. She has cerebral palsy. Her mother carried her for 11 months instead of 9, during which time her brain was damaged. Quite naturally Shelly had a very tough time growing up. She went through both pain and despair. At one point, she was tempted to take her own life. However, she came to a point in her life where she could trust God's grace. Then her disability turned into a wonderful ability—encouraging people not only with disabilities like cerebral palsy but with any misfortune as well. Shelly has become a powerful motivational speaker, whose slurred speech and jerky gestures enhance, rather than diminish, her effectiveness. She leaves audiences spellbound. Every time I hear her speak, I'm not thinking "What a terrific person Shelly is!" but "If God can transform her thorn into such a powerful ministry, what could He do with the thorn I'm dealing with right now?"

So, here's how to look at your problems: each one is a tool for ministry—provided you allow God to solve them. If you work through one problem successfully, by God's grace, you have one tool in your toolbox. If you

You must

present

yourself

to your friend

as a fellow

struggler.

work through many problems, you have an extensive repertoire of helpful wisdom to share.

On a practical level, you must lead from a position of weakness. You must present yourself to your friend as a fellow struggler, not someone who has all the answers. If you come across as having your act completely together, which you don't, you stifle your friend's willingness to open up. However, if you are transparent and vulnerable, you lay the foundation for constructive conversations.

I would offer three words of caution: First, we must never blame God for our misfortune or claim that the terrible thing that happened to us was in itself good. It was not good that Shelly developed cerebral palsy in her mother's womb. It was a tragedy. And God didn't make it happen; it was caused by a natural physical malfunction. Just as Jesus said concerning the man born blind, "Neither this man sinned nor his parents sinned, . . . but this happened so that the work of God might be displayed in his life" (John 9:3).

Second, don't go into details about your moral failures. Paul says in Eph. 5:12, it is a shame to talk about such things. Don't stir up your friend's prurient imagination. It's just better to say, "We all face moral and spiritual battles. Sometimes, we are victorious; sometimes, we're defeated. I must confess that I've lost the battle at times . . ."

Third, don't cheapen grace by thinking of it as a ticket to sin. No, God doesn't wink at sin. He abhors any threat to righteousness, either His or ours, and He makes

His grace available to those who are determined to root sin out of their lives. Admit your failings with the same remorse you felt when you repented of them in the first place.

In the general practice of making disciples, leading from a position of weakness is a helpful tool. There are two special situations in which vulnerable leadership is especially important: when you are dealing with people who have been caught up in sin and when you are dealing with little kids.

The apostle Paul gives very specific instruction about how to help a person who has sinned: "If someone is caught in a sin, you who are spiritual should restore him gently. But watch yourself, or you also may be tempted" (Gal. 6:1). When a businessman is exposed for dishonest dealing or a teenager discovers she is pregnant, this is the perfect time to apply the art of gentle restoration. It demands vulnerable leadership. Many outstanding people have told this same story about a low point in their lives: "When I was in deep despair, embarrassed to death by my own wrongdoing, a wonderful Christian came alongside me and led me back to the Lord."

The sinner knows he or she is guilty and doesn't need to be beaten over the head with more accusations. What that person needs is to get on the path to restoration and a gentle, humble guide to show the way.

Every Christian fails at one time or another; that's why restoration skills are so essential. John Wesley, the great evangelical leader of the 18th century, assumed all Christians would fall at one time or another, so he built into his disciple-making system tools for reclamation. He even included a section in the hymnbook titled "Hymns for Recovering from a Fall."

Another group of people who require vulnerable leadership is little kids. Making disciples of children is the wisest investment a church can make—for obvious reasons:

- More people choose to follow Jesus in childhood than after the age of 15.
- Good character is most easily developed on the foundation of following Jesus.
- The hearts of children are tender.
- Jesus told us to "let the little children to come to me" (Matt. 19:14).

I try to get to church a few minutes early every Sunday so I can talk to the little kids: the 3-, 4-, and 5-year-olds. Why? Because they will be teenagers in 10 years, and I want to be able to talk to them then about serious discipleship.

Last Sunday, I was visiting in a church whose pastor is serious about making disciples. "Where should I start?" he asked.

"How long do you plan to serve this church?" I responded.

"For the rest of my ministry," he said.

"OK, start with the preschoolers—the little kids. Interact with them at every opportunity and lead from a position of weakness."

"How do I do that?" he asked. So I showed him. A little girl was coming out of the sanctuary, holding her daddy's hand. She told me later she was 4 years old. I knelt down and untied my shoe.

"Excuse me," I said to her. "I have a problem. My shoe came untied. Can you help me?"

Even the most shy child will respond to someone in need, someone who is vulnerable. "I can't tie shoes yet," she said, "but my dad can." She pulled him away from a conversation and said, "Daddy, he's got a problem . . ."

That opened the door for a cute conversation with Emily. She informed me that she'll be 5 next year, "and my daddy is 10." She showed me all 10 fingers. We continued to have an interesting conversation. I was careful not to look directly at her: remember, I'm the one who has the problem (my shoe is untied); she is the one in charge, the one giving aid. If she's going to be in a position of strength, I must assume a position of vulnerability.

Why should this pastor learn the art of leading from a position of weakness? Because it is a powerful tool in making disciples. Because people who sin need restoration. And because Emily will soon be a teenager.

## For Reflection and Discussion

1. What is the advantage of leading from weakness rather than strength?

2. What should we not do when talking about our own failures and temptations?

3. How is leading from weakness a good tool for establishing relationships with preschoolers?

4. How would you define *grace*?

5. What is the value of the bad experiences we have had in terms of making disciples?

sixteen

# listening

with

# Your

# eyes

One of the hidden secrets of success is the art of listening. In every area of life, attentive listening will pay handsome dividends. If you are a salesman, your profits will increase dramatically when you learn to hear your customers' inner objections, unspoken desires, and hidden reservations. If medicine or one of the other helping professions is your career, the accuracy of your diagnosis depends on your ability to be a good listener. Even the difficult assignment of parenting depends largely on the skill of listening.

Some years ago I came across a wonderful book by pastoral psychologist John Drakeford titled *The Awesome Power of the Listening Ear.* Dr. Drakeford demonstrates the amazing potential of aggressive and attentive listening. He argues persuasively that listening is the one talent any one of us can learn. The benefits far outweigh the little investment we must make to enhance our ability to hear what's really important.

When I was taking science classes in college, I learned one of those obscure terms freshmen like to bandy about in order to impress their friends. The word is *auscultation,* and it literally means "the science of listening." The doctor practices auscultation when she places her stethoscope on your chest and says, "Breathe deeply." She listens from the outside and hears what's going on inside. "You've got bronchitis," she says. How does she know that? Because she has a finely tuned ear, and she has learned the art of auscultation. What may sound like wheezes and whistles to you, even through a stethoscope, sound like bronchitis to her.

The science of listening is also a critical tool in the practice of making disciples. Following Jesus is first of all a matter of the heart. As you and I invest in redemptive friendships, helping those we love in their relationship with God, we must learn to listen on the outside to what's going on in the heart.

When someone says, "Let's have a heart-to-heart talk," that normally implies a very serious, no-holds-barred discussion. It's the time to deal with very important issues. In a very real sense, every interaction between Christian friends should be a heart-to-heart conversation, because loving God and loving our neighbors are primarily issues of the heart.

Jesus said the greatest commandment is "love the Lord your God with all your heart and with all your soul and with all your mind and with all your strength" (Mark 12:30). Your heart is the center of who you are: your deepest desires, your hopes, cherished memories, dreams, motivations, and affections. It is also the source of your fears, resentments, wrong passions, rebellion, and hurt. That's why King Solomon advised us in Prov. 4:23 to "Keep your heart with all diligence, for out of it spring the issues of life" (NKJV).

When you sit down with your friend, enjoying a cup of coffee or a football game, you need to be able to hear what's going on in his or her heart. According to Scripture a heart may be joyful or it may be grieved. It may be thankful; it may be broken. It may be valiant; it may be wounded. It may be pure; it may be wicked. It may be cheerful; it may be troubled. You can't help your friend if you can't read his or her heart. Only then can you have a heart-to-heart discussion.

Jesus was our model in reading people's hearts. He could look at the crowd who were listening to Him preach and say, "These people honor me with their lips, but their hearts are far from me" (Matt. 15:8). He could walk through a jostling crowd and read the heart of a woman who in faith had touched the hem of His garment.

In normal conversation words often cover up rather than reveal what is actually taking place in the inner man. Only as we fine-tune our listening skills can we get down to the heart of the matter. All successful disciple-makers are great listeners; very few are great talkers.

Your eyes are also listening tools. To engage in powerful conversations you need to listen with your eyes. As you train your eyes to listen, you learn to pick up nonverbal signals from your conversation partner. Total communication demands total awareness.

I had a fascinating discussion with sailor/adventurer Alvah Simon. In his book *North to the Night,* he described the observation powers of an Inuit hunter who accompanied him on a sailing trip through the islands off the coast of Newfoundland. Alvah's untrained eye counted 40 polar bears in one day, but his Inuit friend could give a detailed description of every bear. The difference was one of intense observation: Alvah was a visiting observer, the Inuit was identifying each bear and predicting how it would respond. Why? Because interacting with polar bears on a daily basis is a life-and-death issue.

Making disciples is also a life-and-death issue: spiritual life. The ability to interpret the nuances of nonverbal communication is essential to spiritual formation, because what our friend feels is more important than what is said.

You will remember from your reading of the New Testament that Jesus had a persistent frustration with the people who heard Him preach. "He who has ears to hear, let him hear!" He frequently lamented. In Luke 8:18 He made this intriguing comment: "Consider carefully how you listen. Whoever has will be given more; whoever does not have, even what he thinks he has will be taken from him." What is He talking about here? I believe Jesus was linking attentive listening to any kind of achievement, material or spiritual. To those who learn to listen, more will be given. Those who refuse to pay careful attention, especially to Jesus' words, will lose even what they already have.

One valuable skill is noticing what other people notice. What catches their eyes? Dr. E. Stanley Jones, Methodist missionary to India, used to say, "What gets your attention, gets you." It's important to know what gets your friend's attention, because the eyes reflect the intentions of the heart.

One time a man called and asked me for an appointment to talk about his lack of spiritual growth. "I seem to have plateaued out in my walk with Christ," he said. "Can you help me?" So, I agreed to meet him for lunch and see if I could offer any assistance. As we sat across the table from each other I listened to his words, and they sounded sincere enough. He told me of his decision to follow Christ and the steps he and his wife had taken to develop their spiritual lives. However, as we talked I noticed that his attention was diverted by every woman who walked by. His mouth was saying one thing, but his eyes were saying something else. I sensed that he had a heart problem.

One of my colleagues, James Li, is both a martial arts expert and a minister to junior high kids. One of the skills he learned in his martial arts training helps him communicate with kids. It's what the martial arts people call soft eyes. Having soft eyes means cultivating the ability to take in the whole situation without focusing on one object. It's 360 degree awareness. Soft eyes enables a martial arts expert to comprehend every factor in a confrontation with an opponent, guarding against missteps and taking advantage of opportunities. Soft eyes are essential for effective conversations as well. That skill enables the listener to interpret every nuance of the interaction and respond accordingly.

Listen to the whole person. Take in the whole environment. There is so much more to receive from your friend than just words. He or she will tell you by body language not only what he or she has experienced but also how he or she feels about those experiences. Our memories record past events in stereo: on one track is what happened, on the other is how we feel about what happened, what meaning we attach to the event. One track is as important as the other.

Your eyes are not only telepathic sensors but also facilitators of discussion. You speak volumes with your eyes, perhaps even more than with your words. Appropriate eye contact says to your friend, "I am paying close attention to what you're saying. I'm 100 percent here." You can say with your expression, without a word, "Tell me more" or "I empathize with you" or "I don't fully understand what you're saying."

Poor eye contact can also diminish the effect of conversation. Don't stare, it makes people nervous and gives the impression you're prying into forbidden territory. And don't allow your eyes to flit around the room, looking for someone else to talk to. Both are rude and inappropriate. Your eyes express both acceptance and approval, and there is an important distinction. When you say with your eyes, "I accept you as you are," that gives your friend the privilege of being honest and transparent. Once a foundation of acceptance has been established, your eye messages of approval can say either "Yes, you are on the right track" or "That wasn't the right way to handle things."

One time I was having dinner with a family in their home. The father was seated at the head of the table, and his eight-year-old son was seated next to me. The youngster started to tell a joke: "Did you hear the story about the

. . . ?" Then he quit in midsentence. Nobody else had said a word, but I sensed that he had picked up an eye signal from Dad that meant, "That's not an appropriate story for this setting."

It reminded me of a verse from Ps. 32:8-9 that says, "I will instruct thee and teach thee in the way which thou shalt go; I will guide thee with mine eye. Be ye not as the horse, or as the mule, which have no understanding: whose mouth must be held in with bit and bridle, lest they come near unto thee" (KJV). God directs our way by subtle communications, but only to those who live in such intimate fellowship with Him that we can pick up His eye signals.

God has entrusted to us one of His most precious gifts: a friend. Our response to our Father's generosity should be to help that friend become all he or she can be, by God's grace. The measure of our loyalty and affection for that friend is the lengths to which we will go to listen to the cries of his or her heart.

## For Reflection and Discussion

1. How does a person "listen with his or her eyes"?

2. What is the science of auscultation? How does it apply to the process of making disciples?

3. What kinds of signals do we send with our eyes?

4. How do we discover the condition of our friend's heart?

seventeen

conversion

is

mostly a

Matter of

conversation

Let's face an unpleasant reality: most churches in the United States are not growing. Church attendance as a percentage of the population has been flat or declining for several decades. Very few nonbelievers are becoming genuine disciples. So, why is the powerful message of Jesus Christ and His unshakable kingdom not getting enthusiastic reception in America? Why? Because our church leaders have chosen the wrong methods. They don't work.

In the 1960s some churches thought they had found the perfect method: busing. Pick up kids in poor neighborhoods, offer them prizes and goodies, and trust they will eventually become serious Christians. Sunday School attendance went up for a while, but that method didn't produce long-term numerical or spiritual growth. Then, television evangelism was the big rage. Despite early successes, that method didn't produce growth, either. The past generation has witnessed a plethora of techniques that were supposed to produce church growth: contemporary music, recovery groups, slick promotional ads, big public rallies, gimmicks and contests, conducting church meetings in religion-neutral sites, audiovisual enhancements to worship services, outdoor billboards, and hundreds of other clever devices. With what result? The church continues to languish. The methods aren't working.

One denominational leader lamented, "The population of the U.S. is growing faster than our whole church network. That means we aren't even reaching our own children. We've tried everything, but our membership keeps slipping. What are we doing wrong?"

I asked, "How straight can you take it?"

He responded, "I'm desperate to know the truth. Our church is dying."

Here's what I told him: "The efforts of your denomination remind me of that story in the reign of King David, when God put it in his heart to bring the ark up to Jerusalem and set it in the Tabernacle (2 Sam. 6; 1 Chron. 13). He placed the ark on a cart, drawn by oxen, and headed for Jerusalem. Along the way the oxen stumbled, and the two sons of Abinadab, Uzzah and Ahio, reached up to steady it. When Uzzah touched the ark he was struck down dead, and the whole enterprise came to a halt. David became angry with God that his friend had been killed and the project wasn't going anywhere. So here's my question: where did David get the idea of carrying the ark on a wagon?"

"From the Philistines," he answered correctly. "It had caused so much trouble in their country that they loaded it on a wagon and sent it back to Israel."

"Exactly!" I told him. "David's bungled project is a perfect picture of your denomination: you are certainly God's dear people, and you are sincerely trying to accomplish what you believe to be God's will. But you have borrowed your methods from the Philistines. God gave explicit instructions about how the ark was to be carried (Exod. 25:12-15) so this very thing would not happen. But when you use Philistine methods to do God's work, people get hurt and the whole enterprise breaks down."

Listen: the Bible is not only our message book but also our method book. Why don't we just do what Jesus told us to do: make disciples. And why don't we do it like He did: daily conversations about the kingdom of God with a few close personal friends—right in the context of everyday life.

American church leaders have accepted four major myths about how people become Christians. Those fantasies shape the methods churches use to gain converts—the methods that aren't working. The first myth is that some formula or device can be presented to total strangers who will instantly become converted and begin to follow Jesus. It doesn't happen. Actually, it does happen just often enough to keep churches trying it, but that is the rare exception rather than the general rule. Many surveys have found that most people who accept the invitation to follow Jesus and join a church do so in the context of a personal relationship with a friend or family member who is already a Christian. The reason is simple, obvious, and biblical: it is natural for mature sheep to both produce and nurture little sheep.

Several years ago, I (and several hundred other volunteers) participated in a city-wide evangelism campaign by telephone. We were all trained to call numbers from the phone book, make a quick presentation of a simple plan of salvation, and ask people for a commitment. Thousands of calls were made, and hundreds of people "prayed to receive Christ." We had a joyous celebration. However, one year later a national research organization came to our city to evaluate the long-term success of our telephone blitz. To put it mildly, they rained on our parade. After one year they could not find one person in one church in the entire city who had been converted and added to the membership as a result of our incredible effort.

People make life-changing decisions by discussing the options with people they trust. Today's sophisticated shopper doesn't normally make the decision to purchase a new home or car on the basis of a four-minute sales talk. It requires thoughtful deliberation among all those who will be affected by the decision. Presentations of the gospel that ask for a snap decision are no more effective than one-minute used car sales pitches. If they ever worked at any time in history, they don't work now.

The second myth is that unbelievers can be lured into a church by clever promotions where they will hear the gospel presented by a professional clergyman and respond positively. Again, this happens once in a while, but not often enough to enable the gospel to spread in a natural and spontaneous way. Even when it does, the new believer is usually left to his or her own creativity and initiative to figure out what to do next.

So why do churches keep doing this? Because they have become part of giant religious corporations that are driven by the numbers. Pastors are under enormous pressure to come up with statistics that show growth in membership, income, and attendance. Their climb up the professional ladder demands that they produce a growing church. However, the shortcuts that produce quick increases in those nonbiblical categories (membership, income, attendance) work against genuine Christian growth. And, in the long run, they alienate the people who want to be serious disciples.

One of my former students called to ask me to pray for an upcoming revival to be held in his church. My response: "No, I won't pray for that."

He was shocked. "Why wouldn't you pray that people would be converted?"

I told him, "Here are three good reasons: (1) You don't have any plans to bring those who respond up to full maturity in Christ. (2) The people who are running away from God and need to be converted don't come to revival meetings. (3) You haven't discipled those who made a commitment at last year's revival."

Jesus didn't command sinners to come into the church and be saved. He commanded Christians to go into all the world and make disciples. Jesus didn't just mean that professional missionaries should go to China and Afghanistan, but that every Christian should go to the ball game, the shopping mall, and the places where non-Christian friends hang out. We must go into their world with the deliberate intent to make disciples—right there.

If you were sent by your company to be their representative to Ecuador, you would learn the language, customs, and thought patterns of Ecuadorians in order to sell your company's product. You would figure out which segment of the Ecuadorian population is most likely to use your product, and you would study every aspect of that segment's buying habits. You would do this because you are serious about your assignment. You want to do a good job. You want to give a good report to the people who sent you. Why is it different with the much more important task of making disciples?

One of the tragedies of the modern church life is that its many programs shield believers from the real world. From the time of their conversion, they are gathered into holy huddles, completely separated from the real world. Jesus didn't do this. From the moment He called His disciples to follow Him, He led them into interactions with nonbelievers. He showed them how to be in the world but not of the world. Most contemporary Christians are not even in the world. They move from one church gathering to another without rubbing shoulders with needy people.

I recently helped my own church launch a community service project. The aim was to connect Christians who had material and spiritual resources with those who were needy. Our people were to meet in small groups for study, develop a plan, then go out and serve the people who had needs. I went around from group to group, checking to see how they were doing. To my amazement, I discovered that most of these Christians didn't know any needy peo-

the Great

Commission

starts

with the

command

to "go."

ple. They were willing to help and to give—even sacrificially—but their years of church life had isolated and insulated them from their non-Christian neighbors.

The Great Commission starts with the command to "go"—go into Everyman's world with the good news of the kingdom of God. We can't make disciples if we aren't willing to go where they are. Our model is Jesus, who said to Zacchaeus, "Come down! I'm coming to your house for lunch. We're going to talk about the kingdom" (Luke 19:5, author's paraphrase).

The third myth is a sin-oriented theology. The gospel is presented primarily as a guilt management tool, a means by which sinners who deserve hell can get off free. All they have to do is trust Jesus—which means raising one's hand in a church service or praying the sinner's prayer. In this popular but unbiblical religion, the goal is conversion —a transaction by which a sinner's name is recorded in heaven as a saint. Once a decision is made, the job is done.

The problem with this system is that it bears no resemblance to the message of Jesus or the writings of the New Testament. It grows out of an attempt by fifth-century Christians to explain Christianity in the categories of Greek philosophy, and it has influenced theologians ever since. It is also perpetuated by overzealous evangelists who want to produce immediate results. No, God's offer of salvation is not a transaction, it is a transformation. Jesus did not die on the Cross so people could be guilt-free; He died that they might have eternal fellowship with God. His appeal was not to raise your hand and be saved; He said, "Take up the cross, and follow Me" (Mark 10:21, NKJV). The goal is not conversion, it is full maturity in Christ, full fellowship with Him, full cooperation in His work in the world.

I groan when I hear Christians give their testimonies in terms of sin. It's like a man speaking at his own 25th wedding anniversary talking about all the girls he gave up to marry his wife. "Yes, I remember the day when I forsook all others and took only to her." Get over it, man. Tell me about the quality of your relationship, the family you've reared, the things you've accomplished as a team. Discipleship is no more a system to manage sin than marriage is a system to control adultery.

The fourth myth is that our job as Christians is to plant churches. No, Jesus said, "You make the disciples; I'll build the Church . . . and the gates of hell will not prevail against it" (see Matt. 16:18; 28:19-20). Unfortunately the response of the American Church is, "Thank You, Lord, but we have a better plan: we'll build the churches and make them grow. You're welcome to make disciples in them, but You'll have to take the initiative" (see Matt. 16:18; 28:19-20). The outcome is that we have your church and my church and their church, and the gates of hell are doing fine.

The Church is not our responsibility, it is His. If we assume that burden, as many people do, we are usurping His role as the builder of the Church and we are neglecting the one task He assigned to us. Nowhere in Scripture is there a command for Christians to build churches; central in Scripture is Jesus' command that all of us make disciples. When we stand before Him at the end of time He will not ask how our church grew, but whether we did what He told us to do.

Pastors often tell me, "Well, if I do my job and make the church grow, discipleship will happen." No, it doesn't happen that way. In fact, Jesus promised that just the opposite will happen: when we do our job (make disciples), He will do His job (build the Church).

Here's a case study I give to seminary students: I divide them into two groups to chart a course for accomplishing two different missions. Each group is "given" 10 families, all of whom are Christians. The first group's assignment is to describe what it would take to start with these 10 families and establish a church. The second group's assignment is to make disciples—among the same 10 families. What activities are required to accomplish these two goals? Invariably, the two groups of students come up with two entirely different sets of tasks. The first group finds itself concerned with programs, worship services, style of music, buildings, budgets, parking, and so forth. The second group charts a course around matters of the heart: commitment to Christ, prayer, relationships, personal spiritual practices, applying Scripture to life, and so forth.

Our churches are not growing because our methods don't work. They are based on four foundational fallacies:

1. Strangers will be converted if we present the right formula.
2. Sinners will come to the church and be saved.
3. The gospel is mostly about forgiveness of sin.
4. Our job is to make the church grow.

No, the kingdom of God grows one disciple at a time; disciples are made by their friends, one conversation at a time.

I've made a lifelong study of the process by which raw unbelievers become disciples. It almost never happens in big groups or instant experiences.

## For Reflection and Discussion

1. What is the method by which Jesus made disciples?

2. How do you think people make life-changing decisions? What is the process?

3. How does Jesus' Great Commission apply to the little corner of the world in which you live?

4. Whose responsibility is the growth of the Church? What is our responsibility?

5. How is God's kingdom spreading throughout the world?

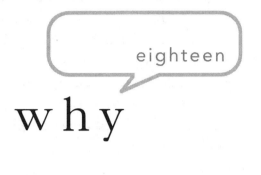

eighteen

# why

should

I do

this?

Making disciples is not complicated, but it can be frustrating, discouraging, and disappointing. There are obvious risks entailed in applying spiritual pressure to friends who are refusing to take the next step. And when friends have problems that need your help, it's often at inconvenient times and could be costly to you. So why should you do this? Why should you invest your best time and energy to helping your friends follow Jesus?

First, we should do this because Jesus told us to do it. You're a follower of Jesus and you want to take the next step. Well, this is it. He said, "Make disciples" (Matt. 28:19), so let's do what He said.

The command to make disciples is the central task of the entire church. There are many other things churches *may* do, but this is the one thing they *must* do. Once the church establishes making disciples as the backbone of its curriculum, every other activity finds its legitimacy in relation to that task.

The Early Church spread quickly from Jerusalem and Antioch, both eastward and westward, transforming lives and communities as it went. As it was said, "The people who have turned the world upside down have come here too." They had no pastors nor church buildings for the first 300 years, yet during that period the growth of the Church was explosive. As Rodney Stark pointed out in his book *The Rise of Early Christianity,* the Church probably didn't spread through mass revival movements or miraculous demonstrations of power but by one believer at a time helping neighbors and relatives take the next step in following Jesus.

I was recently asked by a group of churches if I would help them plant more churches so their denomination could halt its shrinkage. They didn't like my answer. I told them, "No, you already have enough buildings and trained pastors to disciple the entire world, but nothing much is happening in your churches in terms of growth. Besides, planting churches is not our responsibility. Jesus said He would do that. Our job is to make disciples. If we would do what Jesus told us to do, He will do what He said He would do—build His Church. The only problem is, if you make disciples and He builds His Church, it might not have your name on it."

Not only did Jesus commission the Church, as a group, to make disciples, but He challenged His friends to do so individually. After the Resurrection, Jesus met Simon Peter up in Galilee, and He had breakfast with Him by the lake. He looked Peter in the eye and asked him three times, "Do you love me?" You can imagine how embarrassed Peter must have been that Jesus would have to ask him the same question three times. But each time he declared his love for the Lord, Jesus said, "OK, then feed my sheep" (John 21:15 17).

Jesus didn't mean *sheep* sheep. He meant *people* sheep. Peter's personal assignment was to help people follow the Great Shepherd. His mission, as given by Jesus, was to make sure the sheep entrusted to his care didn't stray from following the shepherd, didn't get killed by wolves, didn't drink bad water, or any of the other maladies sheep are so prone to fall victim to. The aim of this book is for you to understand that you have as much a personal assignment from Jesus Christ to make disciples as Simon Peter did.

Some years ago, when I was a college professor, I challenged my students to make disciples, based on this conversation between Jesus and Simon Peter. One of my students took me aside afterward and said, "That was a nice little talk. However, you could strengthen it if you knew the original Greek language. For example, Jesus used two different Greek words for 'love' in this passage and two different words for 'sheep.'"

"Really?" I responded. "How do you know all this?"

"Well," he said, "I'm studying to be a Bible scholar and I've taken two years of Greek and I'm now studying Hebrew. When I finish with advanced Hebrew, I'll get into the other cognate languages of the Old Testament, like Chaldean and Ugaritic and Syriac."

"My goodness," I said. "That's impressive. Maybe you could tell me what kind of sheep He was talking about; were they Suffolks or Rambouillets or Hampshires or some local breed?"

"No," he snorted, "he's talking about people, of course—people who need shepherding."

"And tell me about the verbs Jesus used here."

"They are all simple imperatives," he said.

"Imperatives! That sounds like a command. You mean Jesus actually meant for Peter to do this?"

"Of course."

"And does this command apply to all Christians?"

"Well," he said, "if you knew the principles of hermeneutics, you could make that application, certainly."

"Just one more question: could you share with me the names of some of the sheep you're tending right now, some of the men you're helping to follow Christ Jesus?"

"Well," he said, "I'm a Bible major. I'm not in the Pastoral Ministries department. They study that kind of thing."

"Listen, pal, I hope you get serious about what Jesus told you to do before you have to give a final account of your stewardship. I'm afraid if you had to give an account now, Jesus would ask you, 'What part of "feed my sheep" did you not understand?' and He would ask you in Greek and Hebrew and Ugaritic and Chaldean and Syriac, just so you wouldn't misunderstand the question."

Here's a second reason built on that same conversation with Simon Peter and several other key scriptures: making disciples is the best way to show God we love Him.

"Do you love me? Feed my sheep! Do you love me? Feed my sheep! Do you love me? Feed my sheep!" How much intelligence does it take to see the connection? If Simon Peter really wanted to express his affection and allegiance to Jesus, he had very clear guidelines to do so.

Do you love Jesus? How are you expressing that devotion? By attending church and working in the nursery? By generous giving? By memorizing scripture verses? All those things are good, but they are secondary to the issue closest to the heart of Jesus: the care of His sheep, those friends of yours who are trying to follow Him. Your best means of worshiping Christ is to help your friends follow Him. That brings joy to His heart. The apostle Paul mentioned these first two motivations in his first letter to his friends at Thessalonica, and he added a third one. First he said, we are "entrusted with the gospel" (1 Thess. 2:4*a*). Then he said, "We are not trying to please men but God" (v. 4*b*). Then he added, "because you had become so dear to us" (v. 8). Making disciples is not only the best way to express our love to Christ but also the nicest gift we can give to our friends. Why do we help them follow Jesus? Because we love them so much.

You have a short list of people who are very dear to you. You've sacrificed to make some of them successful in life, like your own children, and you've done your best to show your affection to them. Now you have the opportunity to express your love and loyalty and affection and friendship in the largest dimension possible: encourage them to be all God wants them to be and do.

There's a logistical reason why followers of Jesus should make disciples: it's the best and fastest way to reach the entire world with the good news of the gospel. It's the best and fastest way to extend the kingdom of God. Disciple-building is a multiplication strategy, as opposed to the stodgy addition strategies we are currently depending on.

You learned these illustrations of multiplication in grade school, but let's repeat them:

1.  If you could work for $10,000 a day for 30 days or one penny a day, doubling it every day, which would you choose? The penny, of course. If you chose $10,000 a day, at the end of 30 days your total pay would be $300,000. If you chose the penny, your total pay would be $10,737,418.23, of which $5,368,709.12 would be for the last day alone.

2.  OK, next example: fold a sheet of paper, .01 of an inch thick, 50 times. (Actually you can only fold a piece of paper 7 times, but this is hypothetical.) If you could fold it 50 times, you'd have a stack of paper 444,247 miles thick. That's roughly the distance to the moon and halfway beyond.

3.  How many squares are there on a checkerboard? Sixty-four, last time I played. So if you placed one grain of wheat on the first square, two on the second, four on the third, and eight on the fourth, how many grains of wheat would be on the 64th square? Somebody with apparently too much time on his hands has figured out that there would be enough wheat to cover the subcontinent of India to a depth of 3 feet, 9 inches.

So what does this have to do with the expansion of the Kingdom? Well, if you and I were the only Christians in the entire world, and we wanted to reach the population of the world for Christ, how would we do it? Let's pray together, just you and me, for six months that God would give each of us just one person who would be willing to follow Jesus. Then for the next six months we would each instill in our friends the vision of making one more disciple each in the next six months. At the end of the 1 year there would be 4 of us Christians, at the end of 2 years there would be 16, and at the end of 14 years there would be 5.5 billion Christians, roughly the population of the world. That's multiplication.

So why don't we do this? Because most churches aren't planning to be in business that long. They are not thinking ahead. And most Christians are spectators, not disciple-makers. Even if they do take the initiative and help someone else follow Christ, some efficiency expert will come along and say, "This is so wonderful! Your plan is working so well with ones and twos, let's do this in big classes and programs." No, that's switching back to addition. Besides, you can't make disciples in big flocks and herds; it's a one-to-one process because it is very personalized.

Of course, multiplication is faster than addition, but is it better? Let's go back to Jesus' conversation with Simon Peter by the lake. He said, simply, "Feed my sheep." The principle is this: big sheep not only should produce little sheep but also should nurture and protect them until they can feed themselves and eventually produce their own little sheep.

Many modern Christians have fallen into the delusion that making disciples is the job of religious professionals. Bad thinking! Even in the natural world, shepherds don't produce sheep. Big sheep produce little sheep. And shepherds don't even feed sheep, except when the natural parenting process breaks down. Mama sheep feed baby sheep—their own baby sheep. The shepherd merely leads them into green pastures and beside the still waters so the mature sheep can feed themselves and produce milk for others.

A wonderful revival is taking place in a few churches, more in lands other than America and Europe. Churches are rediscovering the role of leadership in the Early Church, as described in Eph. 4. The role of leaders in the Church (apostles, prophets, evangelists, and shepherding teachers) is not to do the ministry but to equip the believers to do the ministry. This has been called the Equipping Church Movement and is a wonderful return to the pattern of the Early Church. It's a multiplication perspective as opposed to addition.

There's at least one more reason to make disciples, and it's the most important. I've saved the best until last. Here it is: making disciples is the best way to become a disciple. Helping our friends follow Jesus is the surest way to follow Him. Feeding the sheep enables us to become like the Shepherd.

If you have sincerely committed your life to Christ, you share that universal desire of all Christians to become

more and more like the Master. God created us to be con-
formed to His image and never be satisfied until we experience that Christlike heart growing in ourselves. But by
what means, what steps, do we grow to be like Him? By
worship and prayer and Bible study and Christian fellowship and practical service? Sure! All those activities help
shape our spirit. But there is one thing we can do that will
accelerate the formation of Christlike character in us more
surely than any other: making disciples. Feeding the
sheep.

As we become channels of God's grace into the lives
of other people, that same grace also transforms us in the
process. The more we tend God's sheep, the more we become like the Shepherd. The more we help our friends become like Jesus, the more of Jesus' mind and heart we discover in ourselves.

Simon Peter, many years after his encounter with Jesus at breakfast by the lake, wrote to the young Christians
in his church. He told them to do exactly what Jesus had
commissioned him to do: "Be shepherds of God's flock
that is under your care" (1 Pet. 5:2). Then he goes on to
give the reason, that "when the Chief Shepherd appears,
you will receive the crown of glory that will never fade
away" (v. 4).

So what is this crown of glory we are going to receive for feeding the sheep? Is it some piece of headware
we will wear in heaven? No, it is nothing less than the
character of Jesus formed in us. When we see Him, face-

to-face, we will discover to our great delight and His that we have become transformed into His image. How? By the power of His grace as we make disciples. So feed the sheep. It's the best way to become like the Shepherd.

## For Reflection and Discussion

1. What are some of the reasons every Christian should be involved in making disciples?

2. How does the Church grow best and fastest?

3. How can we express our love for Jesus Christ in a way that we know will please Him?

4. What is the reward for investing in "the sheep"?